The Russian Revolution

Dietrich Geyer

The Russian Revolution

Translated from the German by
Bruce Little

BERG
Leamington Spa / Hamburg / New York
Distributed exclusively in the US and Canada by
St. Martin's Press, New York

Published in 1987 by
Berg Publishers Limited
24 Binswood Avenue, Leamington Spa, CV32 5SQ, UK
Schenefelder Landstr. 14K, 2000 Hamburg 55, FRG
175 Fifth Avenue/Room 400, New York, NY 10010, USA

Originally published as *Die Russische Revolution* by
Vandenhoeck & Ruprecht, Göttingen 1977
© Vandenhoeck & Ruprecht
This edition © Berg Publishers Limited 1987

British Library Cataloguing in Publication Data

Geyer, Dietrich
  The Russian Revolution.
  1. Soviet Union—History—Nicholas II,
  1894–1917 2. Soviet Union—History—
  Revolution, 1917–1921 3. Soviet Union—
  Politics and government—1917–1936
  I. Title
  947.08′3   DK258

  ISBN 0–85496–513–0
  ISBN 0–85496–518–1 Pbk

Library of Congress Cataloging-in-Publication Data

Geyer, Dietrich.
  The Russian Revolution.

  Translation of: Die russische Revolution.
  Bibliography: p.
  Includes index.
  1. Soviet Union—History—Revolution, 1917–1921.
  I. Title.
  DK265.G39713 1987   947.084′1   86–31700
  ISBN 0–85496–513–0
  ISBN 0–85496–518–1 (pbk.)

Printed in Great Britain by Billings of Worcester

Contents

Preface

Much has been written about the Russian Revolution and the controversies about what happened in Russia seventy years ago have acquired a history of their own. It is exceedingly difficult, even for a specialist, to acquire an overall view of the mass of sources and secondary literature on the subject; nor is a solid, preliminary overview of this complex subject readily available.

The present volume seeks to offer such an introduction into the history of the Russian Revolution. It is based upon a series of lectures given some twenty years ago at the University of Tübingen. As the lectures were originally conceived, I had decided it would be better not to give a serial, chronological account of events, but rather to concentrate upon a series of key problems. The latter, chosen because of my own personal research interests, included the following:

(1) the social and political preconditions of the revolution, and the crisis of the *ancien régime*;

(2) the interaction of war and revolution, and their significance for the Bolshevik theory of revolution;

(3) the limits and prospects for parliamentary democracy in Russia after the overthrow of the Tsar;

(4) the methods and techniques of Bolshevik revolutionary politics, and the causes of the Bolshevik victory in October 1917;

(5) the early years of Soviet power (up to the separate peace with the Germans at Brest–Litovsk);

(6) the international impact of the Revolution on the history of the present age.

This English edition is based upon the text of the fourth German edition (1985). The selected bibliography has been revised and contains references to more recent scholarly literature in West European languages. An excellent survey of recent tendencies in modern research on the Revolution (especially in Anglo-American scholarship) has been offered in an essay by R.G. Suny, 'Toward a Social History of the October Revolution,' *American Historical Review*, 88, 1983, pp. 31–52), which is to be highly recommended as an updated statement on findings and tendencies in the newer historiography on the revolution.

Dietrich Geyer
Tübingen, January 1987

1

The Old Regime and the Revolution

'The Russian Revolution has yet to find its Tocqueville to make an authoritative statement on the continuities in Russian history right through the violent upheaval of the revolution.'[1] These words, with which Werner Markert opened his contribution to a Festschrift for Hans Rothfels many years ago, are as true today as they were when first penned. Moreover, if one contemplates the present state of historiography and historical research in the Soviet Union, it seems unlikely that a Russian Tocqueville will emerge in the near future.[2] Probably the only work to have become a classic is Trotsky's *History of the Russian Revolution*.[3] Trotsky of course was not a writer or historian who enjoyed the advantages of historical perspective but a man of action who wrote about history because he felt he could still assist in shaping it. The high reputation of his book rests on its very partisanship and his knowledge of the people who participated actively in the events they describe.

Decades later, many of us still feel too close to the Revolution to be able to bridge the gulf between what had been and what was to

1. W. Markert, 'Rußland und die abendländische Welt. Zum Problem der Kontinuität in der russischen Geschichte' in *Deutschland und Europa. Historische Studien zur Völker- und Staatenordnung des Abendlandes. Festschrift für Hans Rothfels* (Düsseldorf, 1951), pp. 293–312; cf. Markert's collection of essays and lectures: *Osteuropa und die abendländische Welt* (Göttingen, 1966), pp. 61–77.
2. For this subject see: D. Geyer,'Gegenwartsfragen der sowjetischen Geschichtswissenschaft' in Geyer (ed.), *Wissenschaft in kommunistischen Ländern* (lectures at the University of Tübingen) (Tübingen, 1967), pp. 259–77, and, more recently, R. Suny, 'Toward a Social History of the October Revolution', *American Historical Review*, 88 (1983), pp. 31–52. Cf. the article by R.D. Warth, 'On the Historiography of the Russian Revolution', *Slavic Review* XXVI (1967), pp. 247–64.
3. L. Trotsky, *History of the Russian Revolution* (3 vols., New York, 1932). Cf. the section 'The Revolutionary as Historian' in vol. 3 of the Trotsky biography by Isaac Deutscher: *The Prophet Outcast* (New York, 1963).

come: old Russia and new Russia were profoundly dissimilar and still cannot be reconciled. To be sure, most of those who were able to say 'we were there' are now dead and those who survive are no longer young. The controversies which swirl about the year 1917 have acquired a lengthy history of their own and monuments are more numerous than eyewitnesses. Nevertheless, time has scarcely tempered the feeling that the Russian Revolution marks a turning point in our century and in ourselves.

There can be no doubt that the October revolutionaries understood their victory as signifying a 'departure from previous history' (A. Weber). Like the generation of 1789 which saw the history of France and indeed of the world 'divided so to speak into two halves' by the Revolution,[4] so the Russian Bolsheviks were convinced that the Russia of the old regime had nothing in common with the new Russia, or at least with what the new Russia was to become. With the Revolution began a new age, a new calendar, a new era in human history; what was past was 'pre-history'.[5] The heirs to the Revolution still cling to this conception. With the October Revolution, it is said, the world entered the era of socialism and Communism. No other revolution in world history can compare with such an epochal event. This message is continually repeated by the Communist Party of the Soviet Union on the anniversaries of the 'Great Socialist October Revolution'.[6]

From a historical point of view, however, it is impossible to accept the notion that all links with the past were severed in 1917. There was continuity within change, as well as an awareness of the continuing presence of the old regime. The past remained part of the present, despite the violent upheaval, and a sense of historical continuity persisted. Indeed, old Russia re-emerged more quickly than the revolutionaries had ever thought possible. Lenin himself discerned its influence, not only in the economic and cultural backwardness of the Soviet Union, but also in the bureaucratic methods of the Soviet state — obviously a creation of the revol-

4. Tocqueville in the foreword to his book *L'Ancien Régime et la Révolution* (1856).
5. The notion of the end of the 'prehistory of human society' appears in the foreword to the 'Kritik der politischen Ökonomie' (1859) in K. Marx and F. Engels, *Werke* (Berlin, 1961), vol. 13, pp. 7–11.
6. For the party 'theses' proclaimed on the fiftieth anniversary of the 'Great Socialist October Revolution' see *Pravda*, no. 187 (25 June 1967). Cf. G.N. Golikov, *Geschichte der Großen Sozialistischen Oktoberrevolution* (transl. from Russian, Berlin, 1962).

utionaries themselves and not a remnant of the *ancien régime*.[7] The opposition which emerged during the 1920s saw in the rule of the bureaucracy, in the party machine's conviction that it was meant to govern and in the use of terror against dissenters a historical legacy which undermined the Revolution and afflicted the new Russia no less than the old. No one succeeded better than Trotsky during his struggle with Stalin in eloquently exposing this fateful condition. It was the context for his development of a 'theory of permanent revolution': Russia could only be liberated from the past, Trotsky asserted, if the Bolshevik Revolution was subsumed within an international revolt.[8]

Russian history intruded on Soviet life in other respects, despite the caesura of the Revolution. After 1930 a Stalin-inspired patriotism, 'Soviet patriotism', began to resurrect old Russia — and not only the superficial features artificially maintained by the party.[9] The new Soviet society taking shape in isolation from the outside world was no longer expected to found its hopes for the future solely on a belief in progress. The new society was now expected to draw reinforcement and strength from pride in Russia's glorious past. This past could not be exploited if revolutionary traditions alone were emphasised. Stalin therefore forbade the denigrating of old Russia as 'a pit of horror and filth'. The oft-lamented tendency towards introversion was no longer described as a national characteristic of all Russians.[10] According to the new teaching, a people is eternal and its culture survives the ages. The achievements of the present were inherent for generations in the best representatives of the people — aristocrats and servants alike. Concepts such as 'people', 'country' and 'homeland' began to bridge customary class-divisions. The Soviet state, which developed into an industrial giant in the course of the 1920s and 1930s, was thus firmly established on the foundations of a glorious imperial history. Some

---

7. Cf. Lenin's last published work which appeared on 4 March 1923 in *Pravda*: 'Better Fewer But Better', *Collected Works*, vol. 33 (Moscow, 1962), pp. 487–502.
8. The best analysis of opposition criticism can be found in E.H. Carr, *The Interregnum 1923–1924* (London, 1954) and *Socialism in One Country* (London, 1959), vol. 2. Besides Deutscher's biography of Trotsky (n. 3), see above all Heinz Brahm, *Trotzkijs Kampf um die Nachfolge Lenins* (Cologne, 1964). Also, R.V. Daniels, *The Conscience of the Revolution. Communist Opposition in Soviet Russia* (1960).
9. For excellent documentation on the historical materials and the problems involved see E. Oberländer, *Sowjetpatriotismus und Geschichte* (Cologne, 1967).
10. J. Stalin to the writer D. Bednyi on 12 December 1930 in Stalin, *Werke* (Berlin, 1955), vol. 13, pp. 21–5.

historical interpretations contained even a hint of Tocqueville, for instance the view that in centralising the state the Muscovite Tsar Ivan the Terrible had laid the mighty foundations of modern Russia.[11]

Russia was great, according to the new wisdom, and the heirs to the old regime, the people of the Soviet Union, were making it greater, more powerful and more attractive than ever. During the 'Great Patriotic War' historians appended to their tales of Soviet patriots and partisans an impressive array of ancestors who had fought for the Russian homeland. The Red Army drew on historical Russian conflicts as a source of military tradition — from Alexander Nevsky and Dimitrii Donskoi, who struggled to throw off the Tartars and push back the Teutonic knights, through to Suvorov, Kutuzov and Nakhimov, the admirals and field marshals of the tsarist era. The victory of 1945 generated a sense of liberation from the shame which foreign aggressors had cast on the former Russian Empire. According to Stalin, amends had even been made for the defeat of 1905 at the hands of the Japanese.[12] So a habit was formed. Today in the Soviet Union patriotism runs strong. It is reinforced by the successes of the present and looks back with pride on the entire history of the motherland.

This harmony of past and present does not escape notice outside Russia, where a belief has long persisted that the old lurks just beneath the surface of the new, that 'Soviet man' does not differ much from the Russian of old. Any transformation is taken to be superficial, as having little impact on the substance of what it is to be 'essentially Russian'. Interpretations such as this are clearly more likely to lead one astray than to shed light. However, as Walter Jens has recently suggested, it is very 'realistic' to focus our attention once again on the old truths: 'Behind Moscow Byzantium looms, in the Bolshoi Theatre the Tsar's box speaks of muted traditions. Beneath the dogmatic surface lurks the counterpart of Roman rationalism — the spirituality of the European east.'[13] This sounds like a well-deserved reproach aimed at those who flatter themselves

---

11. See the article by L. Yaresh in the omnibus volume edited by C.E. Black, *Rewriting Russian History. Soviet Interpretations of Russia's Past*, 2nd revised edn. (Vintage Russian Library V. 738, New York, 1962), pp. 216–32.
12. Stalin's address to the people, 2 September 1945, in J. Stalin, *On the Great Patriotic War of the Soviet Union* (Moscow, 1946), pp. 229–33.
13. W. Jens in a discussion of a work by Wolfgang Kraus (*Der fünfte Stand. Aufbruch der Intellektuellen in West und Ost*, 1966) in *Die Zeit*, no. 18, 8 May 1967, p. 25.

by pointing to the intellectual narrowness of Soviet Russia. However, similar tones often do not sound so edifying when they
emanate from other quarters. Facile comment to the effect that
much has remained the same is often substituted for real thought,
and at times even pungent material is introduced with the intention
of reviving anti-Communist beliefs and anti-Russian or even anti-
Slavic sentiments. The greater the effort — especially in Germany —
to escape from the darkness of one's own history, the easier it is to
ascribe an unchanging nature and historical continuity to the 'East'.
Foreign interpretations of a 'perverted German history' leading
from the Crusaders by way of Luther and Frederick the Great to
Bismarck and finally to Hitler have been summarily rejected, but
this has not always served to root out similar distortions and
prejudices about the continuities in Russian history.[14]

The old dream of world empire cherished by 'Moscow, the third
Rome' is considered to reappear in the guise of Soviet imperialism
or the Communist International. The 'spirit of Bolshevism' becomes a mystical extension of traditional Russian philosophy.
Sometimes the renowned messianism of the East is emphasised,
sometimes the stolid collectivism of Russia's peasant peoples. The
mir system belonging to the old village commune is seen as the
embryo of today's kolkhoz, while the bearded tsars and autocrats of
yesteryear are thought to prefigure the red tsars and autocrats of
today. The propensity of the Russo-Slavic people to become an
easily manipulable mass society is supposedly evidenced by an
indifference to individual freedom. Russia has been left untouched
by Humanism, the Renaissance, the Reformation, even the continuing influence of the ancient world. Scratch Soviet man and you
will find the Russian of old; scratch him a little deeper (as Napoleon
is said to have recommended) and you will discover a Tartar.

Not all views of Russia, old and new, have evinced this kind of
fear and horror, fading gradually into hatred and contempt. Numerous observers have felt great sympathy for their subject and have
succumbed to the spell of what they consider to be 'the East'. Many
marvels have thus been described. Nothing seems more certain or
irrepressible to these people than the famous 'Russian soul' and they
seldom experience difficulty at initiating themselves into its myster-
ies. The profoundest insights into this soul have always flowed from

14. Examples: *Maßloses Rußland. Selbstbezichtigungen und Bezichtigungen*, ed.
Harry Harvest (Zurich, 1949); Dieter Friede, *Das russische Perpetuum Mobile*
(Würzburg, 1959); also W. Keller, *Ost minus West = Null* (Stuttgart, 1960).

the study of Russian authors, especially the most abstruse. Myriad legends echo about the ancient Kremlin and educated dilettantes are not about to cease invoking them in order to expound modern policies.[15]

Rehearsed round many a table and tested in the course of numerous political speeches, these 'insights' survive in easily maintained form — ammunition to be sure for those to whom the 'intellectual and political struggle' never ends but also for those who seek nothing more than the reconciliation which proves so elusive.

Critical or even self-critical thought always reveals that these preconceived ideas bear little fruit and are of absolutely no help in historical research. There is no doubt, however, that the continuing links between old Russia and the Soviet Union are of major importance to historical research. Far from being taboo, the study of continuity in Russian history is seen as one of the most alluring and complex questions facing historians today. Approaching the task *scientifically* implies asking disciplined questions and subjecting one's 'interest in history' (R. Wittram) and one's curiosity as a historian to the scrutiny of the public and oneself. Critical study must be made of views which, while laying claim to intellectual respectability, really amount to nothing more than a stew of superficial tourist impressions, undigested Dostoevsky, picturesque onion domes and movie versions of Pasternak. If we wish to avoid this swamp we must approach our subject with moderation and draw careful conclusions. Questions must be left open if nothing can be said for certain.

What has previous historical research told us about the old regime and the Revolution? What is the place of the watershed of 1917 in former interpretations of pre-revolutionary and post-revolutionary times? Our answer should begin with a general observation, a truth which arises also in respect to the French Revolution. Great revolutions, to an even larger extent perhaps than great wars, influence more than just the times in which they occur; they also have a profound impact on later historians — on their perspective, con-

---

15. In the case of F. Heer such interpretations stream forth as if automatically; see the chapter on Russia in his book *Europa-Mutter der Revolutionen* (Stuttgart, 1964), pp. 730–831. *Emigré* Russian philosophers (Berdyaev or Stepun for instance) played no small part in the spreading of these opinions. A detailed study of stereotypes and their effect on popular views in Russia would be as worthwhile as it is methodologically difficult. A first step in this direction can be found in: W. Laqueur, *Germany and Russia* (New York, 1964) and idem, *The Fate of the Revolution: Interpretations of Soviet History* (London, 1967), as well as in G. Stökl, *Osteuropa und die Deutschen* (Oldenburg, 1967).

cepts and standards. Historians develop a keen interest, not only in the events of the revolution, but also in the historical reasons for those events. As a result, the earlier period is seen as the *pre-history of the revolution*. Those historical trends that did not develop further are ignored. The very term 'old regime' assumes the revolution, and those who employ such a concept are usually referring to the past rather than to life as it is lived from day to day. They therefore have a tendency to view the era *before* the revolution in the light of subsequent events and this means of course as a cause of the revolution.

Our attention therefore focuses on the pre-history of the Revolution, its sources or roots — a fascinating topic for anyone with an interest in history. There is something compelling about observing the old regime as it worked to catalyse the Revolution, not only because of its weaknesses, deficiencies and incompetence but also on account of its attempts to strengthen itself by means of assimilation, suppression and 'timely and well-conceived governmental reform' (Gentz). The history of pre-revolutionary Russia abounds with efforts to renew the state and the social order so that they might withstand the currents of time. Tsarist Russia felt compelled to modernise and adapt. Ever since the eighteenth century this had been the upshot of its place in Europe and its would-be role as a European and world power. *Raison d'état* demanded political and social reform; adaptation and modernisation became imperative.[16] This concern about Russia's position as a great power prompted repeated attempts at renewal — long before the sleep of the Tsar and his loyal subjects was disturbed by intimations of revolution or by the presence of a clear danger. The ruling elite was always concerned however that in deciding to modernise, the old regime might be overstepping its own limitations and so destroying the foundations on which it rested. This is the reason for the troubled relationship which all rulers have with progress. They realise that progress is necessary, but hope that the status quo can somehow be preserved; they know they cannot remain immobile, but feel that in forging ahead they are assisting their worst enemies.

The movement for reform from above received its first strong impetus in the middle of the nineteenth century from the Crimean

16. The term 'modernisation' has supplanted the traditional tendency to speak of the 'Europeanisation of Russia' in recent research, a reflection of the increased interest in social and institutional history. Cf. C.E. Black, *The Dynamics of Modernisation* (New York, 1966).

War, or more exactly from Russia's defeat in that war. The reforms undertaken were unparallelled in their scope and implications. Serfdom was abolished, and with so-called emancipation came an array of liberal institutions: independent courts, a more relaxed censorship and organs of local self-government. 'Public opinion' now emerged and began to influence political decision-making. An attempt was underway to transform the autocratic system from an authoritarian society divided along strict class lines in to a civic society, a modern nation of citizens. As a result, general conscription was introduced and the old army, composed of dragooned souls working off their taxes, was abandoned. The necessary superstructure was created for Russia to adopt new economic methods, with the importation and accumulation of capital and the rapid expansion of industry becoming high government priorities. The chief causes of the Revolution may very well be found not only in the deficiencies of this programme but also in its striking successes.[17]

Half a century later in 1905, the second and final great attempt at internal renewal commenced. The effects of defeat in the Russo-Japanese War had been exacerbated by a dangerous revolutionary convulsion triggered by the war as well as by other factors. If the regime was to survive, it could not be satisfied merely with suppressing the revolution. It would have to change, to renew and regenerate itself if it was to ward off the internal and external threats to its existence. This predicament finally compelled the Russian monarchy to adopt the 'pseudo-constitutionalism' described by Max Weber in 1906 using Russia as an example (though he was fully aware that his critique also applied to contemporary conditions in Prussia).[18] New Fundamental Laws were introduced and a parliament established, though the suffrage was class and property-based and the parliament was assigned only a weak role in the legislative process. Political parties, professional associations and new press organs were permitted, although they were closely supervised. Through incipient land reform an attempt was made slowly to dismantle the old agrarian order whereby peasants were bound to the land, more particularly to the traditional peasant communes. The goal of this reform was to create a market-orientated peasant agriculture able to surmount the permanent agrarian crisis and to

17. For what follows see chapters two and three in this volume.
18. Max Weber, *Rußlands Übergang zum Scheinkonstitutionalismus* (Tübingen, 1906) (*Arch. für Sozialw. und Sozialpolitik* XXIII, supplement).

generate the capital needed for a rapidly expanding industry.

The First World War interrupted many initiatives which seemed to promise success. During this third and greatest catastrophe reform could no longer be attempted, not even political reform. (The Tsar's refusal to grant parliament a stronger constitutional role reveals once again a curious parallel with Prussia.)[19] The revolution which subsequently engulfed Russia swept away much more than just the monarchy — not the only monarchy to be destroyed by the war. The unity of multi-ethnic Russia was lost and a process of disintegration began which a little later also overtook the empires of the Habsburgs and Ottomans. But this was not all. Most important was the destruction a few months later of the provisional democracy which the heirs to the Tsar had set about 'improvising' because their beliefs — their weaknesses as well as their strengths — made other approaches seem impossible. The German Weimar Republic was also an 'improvised democracy' (T. Eschenburg), though it is obvious that the preconditions for such an experiment were very different in Germany and Russia. From these dissimilar preconditions flowed the differences between Red October in Petrograd and November 1918 in Berlin.

Historical research has tested its resourcefulness on these complex problems and it is here, above all, that the pre-history of the revolution is believed to reside. Studies of the 1860s have dealt primarily with the promise and limitations of liberal reform under the Autocracy. They raise the question of whether a genuine opportunity existed, and was then finally squandered, to develop a constitution and the rule of law, to emancipate social relationships and to create a consensus between the state and the developing citizenry. Was the chance already lost during the 1860s of ever achieving a balance between demolition and construction, between the needs of a crumbling agrarian society and the requirements of forced industrialisation? These same questions are posed once again in relation to the second great attempt at reform between 1905 and 1914. Researchers are faced with a collection of complex problems: the interaction between war and revolution, between the labour movement and the revolution, between democratisation and the imperial policies of a great power, between agrarian reform and industrial growth and between urbanisation and rural over-population. The evolution of class-conflict must be examined, as

19. See p. 47ff. in this book.

well as the ability of political institutions to expand and to change. Consideration must also be given to influential social and economic elites and to the role of the monarchy in a multi-ethnic state.

These numerous questions remain the subject of intense controversy among historians. For a short time during the 1950s it seemed that a consensus had emerged — a consensus which failed to acknowledge even to itself its intimate relationship with cold war politics. Historical interest focused time and again on the sole question of whether tsarist Russia really was condemned to destruction. Those who posed the question usually had a ready answer, one which could be couched in a maxim which has a certain truth but which can never be tested. History, it was said with a touch of defiance, is never closed to the future. In other words and with particular reference to Russia, the old regime was prospering, or after 1905 at least, was beginning to prosper and to evolve into a bourgeois–capitalist, constitutional state modelled on Western Europe.[20] Nothing therefore was inevitable. The industrial growth rate was high and land reform was awarding the best and most diligent peasants their due. The liberal middle class was expanding and the small bands of revolutionaries, drawn from the radical intelligentsia, were withering away in self-isolation and factionalism. This intelligentsia, it was said, merely confirmed Toynbee's remark that 'intelligentsias are born to be unhappy'.[21] The beckoning future was not vitiated until the nations of Europe slid into a war which no one wanted — a chance event, an accident of history which finally gave the minority of revolutionary conspirators an opportunity to seize power on the streets. Despite many accurate observations, this view rested on a complacent misunderstanding which became entrenched as the Western response to a rigid historical determinism which proclaimed that the revolution was the inevitable, quintessential outcome of the historical process. The October Revolution proved the accuracy of the laws of history, according to Communist historians, and the laws of history proved the inevitability of the Revolution.

Without succumbing to bland determinism, we now realise not only that history is never closed to the future but that there are also

20. For the origins of this interpretation see the standard views of German specialists on Russia before 1914 (O. Hoetzsch, O. Auhagen *et al.*); evidence in W. Markert, *Osteuropa und die abendländische Welt*, (Göttingen, 1966), pp. 166ff.
21. This quotation from Toynbee is taken from Th. von Laue, *Why Lenin? Why Stalin?* (Philadelphia and New York, 1964), p. 86.

past futures — to modify an idea of Reinhard Wittram[22] — futures which are squandered and lost before we ever reach them. There is much to indicate that research has now set off in a new direction and that different questions are being asked about the Russian Revolution and its causes, more dispassionate questions which reveal greater awareness of the temptation to take an ideological view of problems instead of a cool, analytical approach.[23] Former positions are being abandoned and superannuated phrases revised. The research which gains respect and provides new insights is not overly concerned with tales of the secret service and of the scandals which accompanied the Russian Revolution as surely as many others.[24] Nor does it engage in political analyses based on biographical and psychological details like the many attempts we have seen in the past to discover, for instance, the essence or origin of revolution in Lenin's sex life and in the frustration of many revolutionaries.[25] Interpretations such as these have ceded in the last few years to social and economic analysis. Here a great deal still remains to be done and rich historical mines have yet to be exhausted. Studies which investigate the relationship between society and economics did not appear out of thin air. They demonstrate instead how research into the Russian Revolution has benefitted from methods and approaches which are now re-entering the historiography, having passed through the modern social sciences where they were rigorously tested on different kinds of problems. It is still impossible to treat any single method as the one true way or to replace history with statistics or total national income. However, new methods must be weighed and tested and our historical judgments adjusted to include confirmed results. History clearly cannot be reduced to measurable quantities but some elements of history can be quantified and we need to understand them. Modern structural research, of which more will be said in the final chapter, attempts to

22. R. Wittram, *Zukunft in der Geschichte. Zu Grenzfragen der Geschichtswissenschaft und Theologie* (Göttingen, 1966), pp. 5ff.
23. The works of Leopold Haimson and the discussion which they provoked did a great deal to encourage this transition: 'The Problem of Social Stability in Urban Russia 1905–1917', *Slavic Review* XXIII (1964), pp. 619–42; XXIV (1965), pp. 1–56.
24. Cf. G. Katkov, *Russia 1917. The February Revolution* (London, 1966). This informative work, in which the author does not conceal his monarchist sympathies, blames German agents and money as well as the stupidity of the liberal opposition for the collapse of the monarchy and the February Revolution. Katkov also claims that a conspiracy of Freemasons played a role. Because of the narrowness of his views, Katkov's conclusions are untenable.
25. Stefan T. Possony, *Lenin. Eine Biographie* (Cologne, 1965).

take advantage of these insights.

Research into the causes and results of the Russian Revolution has received new impulses from another source: actual experience of the process of industrial catching up which is now spreading around the world and which in many areas in the so-called 'developing countries' has begun to transform traditional, agrarian societies. Walt Rostow's controversial book outlining a stage theory of economic growth should be seen in this context.[26] Scientific studies of the 'Third World' have engendered new comparative methods and social historians now use them to illuminate historical problems. Modern theoretical insights into the 'infra-structure' of economic development can be applied to economic processes in previous eras.[27] From this point of departure, the notion of treating the Russian experience as that of a 'developing country' gained currency.

These new directions in historical research encouraged some historians to turn away from the revolution in the narrow sense and towards social processes and structures which span the historical watershed of 1917. Particular attention is paid to the remoulding of the social order in Russia, and it is easy to see why this has opened up new areas for comparative studies. The older sociology of revolution, as practised for instance by Crane Brinton at Harvard, concentrated on the comparison of revolutionary processes. It asked who were the Russian Girondists and Jacobins, who was the Russian Bonaparte and when was Thermidor.[28] The more modern type of comparative social history endeavours to derive a typology of modernisation processes. Much longer periods must therefore be studied. This method was successfully applied by Alexander Gerschenkron who examined industrialisation in Russia within the broader European context.[29]

While teaching in the United States, Theodore von Laue continued this approach and arrived at a new understanding of the Russian Revolution. It seemed to him to have been a separate category of revolution, different in structure from its predecessors

26. Walt W. Rostow, *The Stages of Economic Growth. A Non-Communist Manifesto* (Cambridge, Mass., 1960).
27. For the problems which arise see D. Rothermund, 'Geschichtswissenschaft und Entwicklungspolitik', *Vierteljahrsschrift für Zeitgeschichte* 15 (1967), pp. 325–40.
28. Crane Brinton, *The Anatomy of Revolution* (New York, 1938).
29. A. Gerschenkron, *Economic Backwardness in Historical Perspective* (Cambridge, Mass., 1962); C.E. Black (ed.), *Transformation of Russian Society. Aspects of Social Change since 1861* (Harvard University Press, 1960).

in the west, a revolution which came from outside. The course of the Revolution was determined by the need to develop a backward country as quickly as possible: Russia was compelled to catch up with the industrially advanced countries of the West in order to gain a secure place for the Russian Empire in the concert of great powers. Ever since the 1890s when Finance Minister Witte began to promote industrial development, the modernisation problem had been a clear priority dominating the destinies of the Empire. The Bolsheviks felt obliged to assume this traditional burden and they explored possible solutions during the period of war communism and the 'New Economic Policy'. A means of attaining Russia's goal of economic development did not emerge, however, until the technical and economic 'revolution from above' imposed by Stalin in the late 1920s.[30] The expanse of time covered by von Laue makes him a new kind of Tocqueville, if one will, a historian who sees continuity in Russian history much more in the problems posed by industrialisation than in the centralised, bureaucratic state. In any case, this approach casts new light on many familiar questions: the old regime's chances of survival, the reasonableness of its economic and social policies and the alternatives it might have considered.

In the 1930s, and at the cost of tremendous sacrifices, Stalin finally achieved Russia's goals for industrialisation by means of authoritarian compulsion, central planning and the total mobilisation of human resources. Does this mean that the path of the market economy taken by tsarist ministers Witte and Stolypin could lead under Russian conditions only to mass rural poverty and overpopulation? Was the approach which the Soviet Union adopted under Stalin the only one possible? The questions are legion while recent answers remain controversial and full of weaknesses. Walt Rostow arrived at a positive analysis of the chances for success of the market economy approach to the industrialisation of Russia. He inclines to the view that the success of the market economy and entry into the 'take-off' phase has been proven and assumes that the revolution of 1917 interrupted a ripening process which was already bound to bear fruit. More recent studies have energetically contradicted Rostow's argument, as well as his quantifying methodology. They point

30. Th. von Laue, 'Die Revolution von außen als erste Phase der russischen Revolution 1917', *Jahrbücher für Geschichte Osteuropas* 4 (1956), pp. 138–58; Laue, *Why Lenin? Why Stalin? A Reappraisal of the Russian Revolution, 1900–1930* (Philadelphia and New York, 1964). See also the well-balanced analysis of L. Kochan, *Russia in Revolution 1890–1918* (London, 1966).

to the historical and natural constraints operating in Eurasia and marshal economic data to indicate that experiments with a market economy were doomed to failure. The solution sought by the Soviet regime towards the end of the 1920s was therefore reasonable, at least from an economic point of view. However, even this conclusion cannot explain everything. Beyond all the theorising and the data, we are still entitled to revolt as human beings against any talk of Soviet rationality given the tremendous cost in human lives.

Consequently additional questions arise beyond the realm of what can be proven by scientific means, questions which are no longer directed at the Revolution itself but at the generations which succeeded it. Not everyone wishes to be reminded that the shadow of the dead still hangs over revolutionary celebrations in the Soviet Union. Does this mean, however, that those who applaud the Revolution should be impugned? Are we to consider revolutionary eras to be the illegitimate children of history? Or has the Revolution legitimised itself through its descendants? Those who do not hesitate to question beyond the methods which our discipline can bear find that every answer generates new questions.

2

Social Preconditions of the Revolution

When the old regime finally collapsed, few people in Russia could have remembered a time when there had been a feeling of security, of unbroken confidence and faith. To say when 'the good old days' actually were was perhaps even more difficult in Russia than elsewhere. This was true not only of those for whom revolution had become a sustaining hope or even a profession but also of those who saw revolution as the end of all hope. For successive generations in the nineteenth century fear of — or hope for — revolution became ever more deeply entrenched in both the public and private consciousness. People grew accustomed to living with such fears and hopes, much as we have learned, it is said, to 'live with the bomb'. Under Tsar Nicholas I (1825–55) and before the Crimean War, it had still seemed possible that Russia would be spared the convulsions that continually shook the west after 1789.[1] Such hopes began to fade, however, under Nicholas's successors. Tsarist Russia lost forever its role as policeman of Europe and bulwark against the forces of violent disintegration and continual change. Even those who believed that autocracy was the will of God suspected that the traditional order would not last. Under Nicholas, revolution had still been perceived as a foreign problem which occasionally slipped into Russia because of the agitation of misguided *niveleurs* and 'doctrinaires'. Now, however, the horrid threat seemed to emanate from deep within Russia itself.[2]

When the government of Alexander II (1855–81) decided to seek vigorous renewal through reform, the abolition of serfdom and the dissolution of the old feudal order, fears and forecasts of revolution

1. Cf. S. Monas, *The Third Section. Police and Society in Russia under Nicholas I* (Cambridge, Mass., 1961).
2. The widespread fear of revolution in Russia deserves a study of its own.

proliferated. Such sentiments would never again be dispelled.[3] The imminent collapse of the old regime became an article of faith — and not only conspiratorial circles which had sworn death to the Autocracy. Many who considered themselves pillars of the old order felt revolution to be an ubiquitous presence, a historical inevitability. Tsar Alexander II was himself motivated by fear, and increasingly came to be seen as the Russian counterpart of Louis XVI. There was a widespread feeling that the decision to reform Russia had opened the door for the revolution itself to take a place in the circle of ministers and to dine at the Tsar's own table.

The fountainhead of the mischief was thought to be those liberal Petersburg bureaucrats whom even Bismarck described as 'reds'. By means of their projects and laws they seemed determined to overthrow traditional Russia. The impending catastrophe was presaged by the attitude of the student youth; by their rebellion against 'cultivated society' and everything which deemed itself good, by their anarchistic views and nihilistic pallor. Cigarette-smoking girls from good backgrounds cut off their pigtails and renounced all *contenance* while their male counterparts developed a fateful predilection for 'going to the people' and educating them in the belief that Russia was destined for a historic revolution.[4] Fears of impending revolution were confirmed by glimpses of Russia's new rural citizenry: the coarse, unkempt peasant masses. Rebelliousness was replacing the old servility, making life in the countryside increasingly unpleasant and often insufferable for the nobility. The old security had disappeared. In March 1881 the Tsar-Liberator fell to a terrorist bomb like hunted quarry — the inevitable conse-

3. There is no modern study providing an overall analysis of the reforms under Alexander II. For informative surveys see W.E. Mosse, *Alexander II and the Modernization of Russia* (London, 1958); H. Seton-Watson, *The Russian Empire 1801–1917* (Oxford, 1967), pp. 332–429. For the emancipation of the serfts see T.G. Robinson, *Rural Russia under the Old Regime* (New York, 1932); P.A. Zayonchkovskii, *Otmena krepostnogo prava* (The abolition of serfdom) (Moscow, 1958); Zayonchkovskii, *Provedenie v zhizn' krest'yanskoi reformy 1861g.* (The implementation of peasant reform) (Moscow, 1958). For the agrarian and social background see J. Blum, *Lord and Peasant in Russia* (Princeton, N.J., 1961).
4. For the 'populist' movement (*narodnichestvo*) see the authoritative presentation of Franco Venturi, *Roots of Revolution. A History of the Populist and Socialist Movements in 19th Century Russia* (New York, 1960) (original Italian edition: Turin, 1952); also the assessment of P. Scheibert, 'Wurzeln der Revolution', *Jahrbücher für Geschichte Osteuropas* 10 (1962), pp. 323–36.
5. For a detailed examination of the years of crisis between 1878 and 1882 see P.A. Zayonchkovskii, *Krizis samoderzhaviya na rubezhe 1870–1880-kh gg.* (The crisis of the Autocracy) (Moscow, 1964); cf. the observations and views of the German ambassador: L. v. Schweinitz, *Denkwürdigkeiten* (Berlin, 1927).

quence many felt of times that were out of joint.[5] In view of the gravity of this mood, we are compelled to wonder if continual change and fear for the future had induced a state of self-hypnosis in traditional society, or if this society really was justified in thinking Russia to be in imminent danger of revolution.

The heir to the throne, the phlegmatic Alexander III (1881–94), tried to arrest the course of history. He summoned to his side men of the old stamp who would restore autocratic authority and return His Majesty's loyal subjects to their former passivity. The entire arsenal of the bureaucratic, authoritarian state was mobilised in order to smash the revolutionary circles, blunt the thrust towards constitutional reform and expose liberal impulses as mere phantoms. Governmental activity assumed the aspect of a regressive security police intent on disciplining unruly elements and restraining the emancipation of society and its institutions. The Tsar's vassals would not be allowed to transform the state into an institution of self-governing, mature citizens. The people's desire for political participation would be offset by displays of glamour and prestige on the part of an autocracy representative only of itself. 'Public opinion' would be an artificial creation of the government censor. The public might be permitted upon occasion to applaud official nationalism and the desire of the established minorities to create a powerful national state, but it would never be allowed to express its opinion on self-determination.[6]

Nevertheless the feeling of security, of living in a firmly established order, never did return. Even reactionary policies could no longer escape a dilemma which henceforth dogged all the efforts of the old regime: even during periods of political reaction, social forces which depended not on the status quo but on speedy but profound changes in the traditional order had to be promoted. Russian Marxists had genuine cause for confidence as they surveyed the consequences of industrialisation after the 1880s. By assisting the development of capitalism, the Tsar's finance ministers seemed increasingly to become the inadvertent accomplices of the revolutionaries. Thus, even the servants of the Tsar were condemned to serve the revolution.[7] From the very beginning, the Russian state

6. For a basic analysis see Hans Rogger, 'Reflections on Russian Conservatism 1861–1905', *Jahrbücher für Geschichte Osteuropas* 14 (1966), pp. 194–212; also E.C. Thaden, *Conservative Nationalism in 19th Century Russia* (Seattle, Washington, 1964).

7. A.P. Mendel, *Dilemmas of Progress in Tsarist Russia* (Cambridge, Mass., 1961);

had promoted industrialisation for the sake of its conception of the national interest. Railways were constructed, industrial growth was encouraged and attempts were made to overcome economic backwardness all for reasons of state. The government was the driving force behind modernisation, while military strategy determined the goals, the pace and the urgency of development. The motives were clear: Russia could not simply forgo the political rivalries and involvements of the great powers. In an imperialist age, Russia could not remain at an economic level that more closely resembled its Asian sphere of interest than the modern, expanding economies of those powers which it wished to rival for a place in the sun. Sergei Witte, who initiated the 'industrial revolution' between 1892 and 1902 understood better than any other minister at the time that the Empire was condemned to forward movement, to progress, and that the price of progress was likely to be dangerously high.[8]

The costs of modernisation could not be paid for by Russia's fledgling industries if they were to continue their rapid expansion. They could not generate sufficient investment capital, and industrial production or exports could not cover the payments on foreign loans. 'Primary accumulation' had to be derived from other sources, from financial policies backed ultimately by the taxpayer. This meant that millions of Russian peasants were compelled to bear the costs of industrial progress. The results were horrendous. The volume of state monies required was not overshadowed by private bank capital until the decade before 1914. Any discussion of the social conditions which preceded the Russian Revolution must take this aspect of modernisation into account.

Too much would be glossed over if one were simply to state that peasant agriculture was incapable of generating capital by means of the market mechanism. From the start of the 1890s (at the latest) Russia experienced a permanent agrarian crisis, evidenced by mass

---

R. Kindersley, *The First Russian Revisionists. A Study of Legal Marxism in Russia* (Oxford, 1962); S.H. Baron, *Plekhanov: the Father of Russian Marxism* (Stanford, 1963).

8. The standard monograph is by Th. von Laue, *Sergei Witte and the Industrialization of Russia* (New York and London, 1963). For the problems and an outline of industrialisation and social change in Russia see the contributions in C.E. Black (ed.), *Transformation of Russian Society* (Cambridge, Mass., 1960). The most recent review of Soviet research and the approaches it is taking can be found in P.A. Khromov, *Ekonomicheskoe razvitie Rossii* (The economic development of Russia) (Moscow, 1967), pp. 277ff.; a work available in English translation is: P.I. Lyashchenko, *History of the National Economy of Russia to the 1917 Revolution* (New York, 1949).

poverty, starvation on a vast scale and recurrent catastrophe. The misery was so intense that newspaper readers of the time must have experienced the same sense of horror we feel today when the media report on mass starvation which continues, despite government aid and well-publicised public campaigns.

The origin of Russia's woe was easy to discover: it derived from the emancipation of the serfs. On the tiny pieces of land redeemed by the village communes after 1861 lived a population whose birth rate was the only rapidly expanding factor in Russian agriculture. As elsewhere, emancipation produced a tremendous population increase[9] and from liberation sprang a surplus which no one could manage. The 'demographic revolution' was at the root of the widespread misery. The wretched peasant holdings could not even cover the needs of the rapidly expanding families which lived on them and millions of surplus mouths went hungry.

The government proved unable to develop a programme that could check or mitigate the suffering until after the turn of the century. The limited financial resources of the state had already been committed for years to come, while the revenue from taxes imposed on agriculture did not flow back to the villages. Industry's demand for labour brought no noticeable relief to the great rural areas of Russia. In fact, industry increasingly undercut and destroyed the widespread system of cottage industries. The peasant became the starving competitor of the factory, unable to pull himself by the bootstraps out of his wretchedness. If peasant agriculture was to have an opportunity to flourish, many profound and costly structural changes would have been necessary.

At the beginning of the present century, mass peasant disturbances broke out over wide areas of the Empire, focusing attention on the explosiveness of the situation. Many solutions were proposed. The most radical emanated from the theoreticians of the socialist parties whose programmes were predicated on the violent overthrowal of tsarism, the transition to a democratic republic and, ultimately, to socialism. In the populist tradition, the rural intelligentsia within the Socialist Revolutionary party argued in favour of the full 'socialisation' of land and soil — whatever they and their listeners may have understood by that term.[10] The land, they

9. Population statistics can be found in A.G. Rashin, *Naselenie Rossii za 100 let (1811–1913gg.) (Moscow, 1956).*
10. See O.H. Radkey, 'Chernov and Agrarian Socialism before 1918' in J. Simmons (ed.), *Continuity and Change in Russian and Soviet Thought* (Cambridge,

argued, should be treated as social property and handed over for the perpetual use of those who actually worked it. It was assumed that the peasants' own hopes for the future were compatible with socialism and that the Russian *muzhik* was totally averse to private property and individual initiative. However, such firm beliefs were rooted more in the solipsism of these intellectuals than in down-to-earth familiarity with peasant life. Well before Lenin took power, these utopian dreams had been totally dispelled by the peasants themselves.

More realistic views could be found among the Social Democrats, at least in relation to what their programme had to say about the role of the forthcoming 'bourgeois revolution' (in the Marxist understanding of the term).[11] 'Bourgeois democracy', it was argued, would eliminate the remnants of feudalism in the agrarian order and pave the way for class struggle in the villages. In drawing this conclusion, the Social Democrats were depending on the classical thesis that the development of capitalism would necessarily complete the ruin of the small peasant economy and that the peasant would have to become a proletarian before the rays of freedom could reach him. For a long period, the party wrangled internally about the forms which state intervention would take and about the formula to be applied to the nationalisation of the land. Not until 1905 did the Social Democrats agree to extend their minimum demands to the division of the large estates. They finally decided in favour of this 'petit-bourgeois' formula, in Marxist parlance, in order to gain at least a foothold among the peasant masses. Nevertheless, the basic agrarian programme of the Social Democrats failed even at this point to offer the peasants more than what the Russian liberals — the Constitutional Democrats — were prepared to concede. Around 1905 the latter also began considering reforms which required massive state intervention in the property rights of large landowners. The conviction that dividing up the large estates and the latifundia could help solve the problems of land-hunger had gained currency in these 'bourgeois' circles too,[12] although a view

Mass., 1955), pp. 63–80; also D.W. Treadgold, *Lenin and his Rivals. The Struggle for Russia's Future, 1898–1906* (New York, 1955).

11. D. Mitrany, *Marxismus und Bauerntum* (Munich, 1956); L.H. Haimson, *The Russian Marxists and the Origins of Bolshevism* (Cambridge, Mass., 1955); D. Geyer, *Lenin in der russischen Sozialdemokratie* (Cologne, 1962); J.H.L. Keep, *The Rise of Social Democracy in Russia* (London, 1963).

12. For the Kadet programme of 1905–6 see D.W. Treadgold, *Lenin and his Rivals.*, pp. 191ff.; for the historical background, V. Leontowitsch, *Geschichte des*

such as this threatened to distract attention from the fundamental structural problems in agriculture.

Agrarian experts, responding to a professional understanding rather than to party programmes, favoured a different approach. According to them, land reform was a long-term developmental problem and its capital needs would have to be weighed against those of industry. This consideration alone made it impossible to divide up the large estates, geared towards exports, and rely instead on the productivity of small peasants holdings. Reform (in this view) should start with the dissolution of the village communes, the traditional agricultural order with its system of collective property and joint liability. Pieces of land which were scattered among various villages would have to be rigorously rounded off, each individual farmer's property would have to be consolidated and rationally sized economic units would have to be created by reallocation, resettlement and colonisation. Last but not least, everything would depend on generous credit policies which would encourage the economic initiative of enterprising farmers and help in the transition from extensive to intensive farming.

This became the approach adopted by the government of Prime Minister Stolypin[13] and initial measures were immediately introduced in 1906. Reform was not undertaken for its own sake but because of pressure from the revolutionary movement and the political crisis. Liberal economic theories and traditional bureaucratic paternalism competed with each other in shaping the experiment. We should not overlook the fact that the extensive body of rural reform elaborated by 1910 was of a very high calibre; an ambitious attempt at modernisation without parallel outside Russia. Today these reforms still mark an important stage in the history of agricultural science, though they failed to leave much of an impression on the history of Russia. It was evident that several decades would have been necessary before this gigantic restructuring of the traditional agricultural order could have succeeded in eliminating

Liberalismus in Rußland (Frankfurt, 1957); G. Fischer, *Russian Liberalism. From Gentry to Intelligentsia* (Cambridge, Mass., 1958).

13. Contemporary views and studies include M. Sering (ed.), *Aus Rußlands Kultur und Volkswirtschaft* (Berlin, 1913); K.A. Wieth-Knudsen, *Bauernfrage und Agrarreform in Rußland* (Munich, 1913); W.E. Preyer, *Die russische Agrarreform* (Jena, 1914). The authoritative Soviet monograph is by S.M. Dubrovskii, *Stolypinskaya zemel'naya reforma* (Stolypin's agrarian reform) (Moscow, 1963). For a useful overview see L.A. Owen, *The Russian Peasant Movement 1906–1917* (London, 1937); for internal colonisation: D.W. Treadgold, *The Great Siberian Migration* (Princeton, 1957).

mass rural misery and in developing a healthy, private economy in the countryside. There are many indications that success was not assured, even if world war had not intervened and totally reordered Russia's priorities.

Firstly, we cannot be certain that the government would have been equal in the long run to its self-imposed task. There was no guarantee that the reforms could be financed over the long term. These doubts are justified in view of the state's chronic shortage of capital, its heavy foreign debt and its desire to match the imperial policies of the great powers — policies which obliged Russia to attempt to keep pace in the arms race and increase its rate of industrial growth. Russia's twin economic goals depended on one another: agrarian reform could not succeed without support from a rapidly expanding industrial sector and industrial growth could not occur without rapid success on the agricultural front. After 1905 the banks financed most industrialisation, but it would have been difficult to persuade them to allocate substantial loans to agriculture. The restructuring of rural society increased the risk of new political crises and social disturbances. Reform in the shape of 'revolution from above' increased the danger that the regime would finally destroy itself in its attempts to transform society.[14] No one can say whether the government of Nicholas II would have succeeded in mastering the problems of rural overpopulation and mass poverty among the peasantry. Certainly the parliamentary governments and their authoritarian successors in south-eastern Europe and the eastern part of Central Europe met with little success in their endeavours after the war.[15] One should also remember that Russia's involvement in the First World War was not fortuitous. The regime included war in its political calculations and these calculations cannot be neatly divided into internal and external affairs. Russia's goals for internal development were inextricably linked with her interests and ambitions as a great power. There is therefore no justification for ignoring the government's foreign

14. See the analysis of J. Nötzold, *Wirtschaftspolitische Alternativen der Entwicklung Rußlands in der Ära Witte und Stolypin* (Berlin, 1966). For the controversy about the reform's chances for success see G.L. Yaney, 'The Concept of the Stolypin Land Reform', *Slavic Review* XXII (1964), pp. 275–93; W.E. Mosse, 'Stolypin's Villages', *The Slavonic and East European Review* XLIII, no. 101 (June 1965), pp. 257–74.

15. M. Sering (ed.), *Die agrarischen Umwälzungen im außerrussischen Osteuropa* (Berlin–Leipzig, 1930); W. Conze, 'Die Strukturkrise des östlichen Mitteleuropa vor und nach 1919' *Vierteljahreshefte für Zeitgeschichte*, Jg. 1 (1953), pp. 319–38.

policy when judging the chances that reform would succeed. To say that the reforms failed because of the First World War is not to introduce an extraneous element.[16] The project for internal renewal had always run the risk of political catastrophe.

So far as the social preconditions of the revolution are concerned, it should be noted that agriculture in Russia was in the midst of profound change when the First World War broke out. More had been done to dissolve and cast doubt on the old than to construct the new. Continuing poverty in the countryside, dissolution of the traditional way of life, the transition towards a novel set of circumstances and social misery all conspired to render the Russian masses highly prone to elemental, anarchistic upheavals. The situation was dangerous even though the peasantry had not yet developed a political leader of its own, let alone a broad political consensus.

The working-class problem in Russia was much less atypical than the agrarian problem. Unlike the situation in the West, the working class here was a product of state intervention. Protectionism had been necessary for the industrialisation of Russia and Russian factories never quite lost their character as state institutions.[17] Nevertheless, the plight of Russia's industrial centres looked in its severity and implications much like the social situation which had been seen elsewhere during the early phases of the industrial revolution. Social scientists and socialist educators had already detailed the horrors of capitalism and often continued to do so even though many workers in the West were now more interested in full integration with bourgeois capitalism than in liberation from it. Compared to the massive agrarian crisis, the problems of Russian workers seemed to concern a small minority, even though it was concentrated in the capital cities and in a handful of industrial centres. By the time of the First World War, factory workers in the Russian Empire still numbered little more than three million.

Anyone familiar with the suffering endured by the vegetating peasant masses must have viewed the social ills accompanying Russian industry as insignificant or at least as manageable. The government long clung to the belief that good policing, together

16. See the comments of Hans Rogger, 'Russia in 1914', *Journal of Contemporary History*, vol. 1 (1966), no. 4. Harper Torchbooks 1306, pp. 229–53.
17. See R. Bendix, *Herrschaft und Industriearbeit. Untersuchung Über Liberalismus und Autokratie in der Geschichte der Industrialisierung* (Frankfurt, 1960), as well as the older work of M. Tugan-Baranovsky, *The Russian Factory in the Nineteenth Century*. Translated from the third Russian edition (1907) by Arthur and Clara S. Levin (Homewood, Ill., Richard D. Irwin, 1970).

with the patriarchal protection afforded by the labour laws, would suffice in controlling the labourers streaming from the countryside into the cities and in keeping the small numbers of Social Democrats out of the factories.[18] The plight of industrial workers was seen by and large within the context of the mass misery afflicting the countryside. The government felt that large factories and cities were more easily managed than the rural areas — that vast expanse of provinces which the ponderous Russian bureaucracy still had difficulty in penetrating. In the 1870s and 1880s the majority of workers in the rapidly expanding industrial centres had not yet developed a proletarian class-consciousness likely to be perceived as a threat. The peasant mentality still predominated and many workers retained close links with their rural roots.

For this reason, many of the customs and experiences associated with village life did not disappear when the peasants became industrial workers. Familiarity with elected elders, with communal meetings and decision-making, with joint responsibility, with the old forms of local authority and with the importance of having one's interests strongly represented all stood factory workers in good stead when they attempted to create a collective life for themselves and organise self-help groups. From these origins tiny, rudimentary labour organisations sprang up in workshops and mass housing units. Conflict with factory management spurred them on to probe further. So when contemporary observers write of how huddled masses of humanity were degraded into beasts of burden and offered up to capitalist exploitation, one should realise that these beasts were astonishingly well organised and fully capable of articulating their interests. They might submit to their collective fate, but they also knew how to mount collective resistance. By the 1880s small groups of experienced workers hungry for knowledge began to associate. These circles became acquainted with Marxist

18. For the beginnings of labour legislation see H. Neubauer, 'Alexander II. und die Arbeiterfrage', *Ostdeutsche Wissenschaft* VII (1960), pp. 109–26; for the period which followed, P. Meschewetski, *Die Fabrikgesetzgebung in Rußland* (Tübingen, 1911); K.A. Pashitnow, *Die Lage der arbeitenden Klasse in Rußland* (Stuttgart, 1907); more recent studies include J. Walkin, 'The Attitude of the Tsarist Government to the Labor Problem', *American Slavic and East European Review* XIII (1954), pp. 163–84; Th. von Laue: 'Tsarist Labor Policy, 1895–1903', *Journal of Modern History* XXXIV (1962), pp. 135–45; 'Russian Labor between Field and Factory', *California Slavic Studies* III (1964), pp. 33–65; 'Russian Peasants in the Factory', *Journal of Economic History* XXI (1961). For a Soviet view see A.F. Vovchik, *Politika tsarizma po rabochemu voprosu v predrevolyutsionnyi period, 1895–1904* (Tsarist policies on the labour question during the pre-revolutionary period) (Lvov, 1964).

literature, and trade union or social democratic attitudes and reactions developed. These new experiences could easily have merged with older types of organisation inherited from the countryside.[19]

In this way the Russian factory proletariat drew closer to the methods employed by the labour movement in the West. The strikes of the 1890s demonstrated that the Luddite stage of blind revolt had already been surpassed and that economic demands could be formulated and reinforced with disciplined campaigning. The labour movement was clearly evolving very rapidly in Russia. One should not, however, underestimate the difficulties associated with self-directed proletarian activity in Russia. As long as the bureaucratic police-state forbade all freedom of association and denied workers the right to associate and to strike, the only public indication of the young movement's strength was the illegal resistance which it offered. However, even limited labour conflict over increased wages or minor improvements in working conditions took on added significance because of its illegality. These struggles immediately became *political* — a fact which was underlined by the presence of police and detachments of Cossacks at factory gates.

It is difficult to determine how important a role was played in these developments by the Social Democrat intelligentsia, which had organised into secret cells. The relationship between the intelligentsia and the workers is still a source of controversy.[20] Revolutionary circles certainly struggled with great courage and resolve to end their isolation, to meet with factory workers and to inform them of their historical destiny. The revolutionaries were anxious to show the proletariat how to transform the economic struggle into political struggle — into revolutionary action directed against tsarism and the ruling classes. Without a doubt the government perceived this to be a great danger and did its utmost to prevent the 'revolutionary bacillus' from infecting the factories. The upshot was bitter rivalry between the tsarist secret police and the secret committees of the Social Democratic Party. Both were intent on acquiring control of the working class and preventing their opponent from gaining prestige and the confidence of the working class. The police wished to preserve the social foundations of a tightly controlled,

19. For this and what follows see the works on Russian Social Democracy mentioned in n.11.
20. See R. Pipes, *Social Democracy and the St. Petersburg Labor Movement, 1885–1897* (Cambridge, Mass., 1963), as well as the testy response from the Soviets: R.A. Kazakevich and F.A. Suslova, *Mister Paips fal'sifitsiruet istoriyu* (Mr. Pipes falsifies history) (Leningrad, 1966).

authoritarian regime (in 1903 Zubatov, the Moscow chief of police, even created a legal labour party),[21] while the Social Democrats wanted to claim the working class as the social basis of the revolution. Even before the revolutionary disturbances of 1905 created an entirely new situation, it seemed unlikely that the police state would emerge victorious in this competition with the revolutionaries.

It is true of course that the Social Democrats did not succeed in establishing their party as the leading organ of the proletarian movement, able to foment labour unrest at will. Social Democrats remained in the embarrassing position of being a small, introspective minority. In addition, they had to face competition for the support of factory workers from the Socialist Revolutionaries, who exerted strong influence in many areas of the country. However, no *other* political force existed which could have given the Russian proletariat a modern orientation, no other force which could have hoped to attract the attention of class-conscious workers. The consequences of this first became evident in the revolutionary confusion of 1905.[22] The political crisis of the old regime demonstrated that the 'fusion of socialism and the labour movement' forecast by Marxist theory might have occurred if the political situation had been freer. The proletariat seldom acted under the direct leadership of the Social Democratic Party, but Social Democrat slogans and programmes almost always exerted a strong influence. No revolutionary had foreseen or even imagined the way in which proletarian resistance actually organised itself in 1905, when councils ('soviets') surfaced spontaneously. However, the political and economic demands formulated in these soviets bore an unmistakably socialist stamp: the eight-hour day, social security provisions, the entire catalogue of democratic freedoms and pleas for a democratic republic. In January 1905 icons and pictures of the Tsar had still accompanied the mass petition before the Winter Palace in Petersburg but the red flag soon replaced them at workers' meetings, demonstrations and strikes.

While under duress the Autocracy was obliged to grant a number of concessions which appeared in the October Manifesto and the

21. K. Tidmarsh, 'The Zubatov Idea', *American Slavic and East European Review* XIX (1960), pp. 335–46.
22. A selection of the (abundant) literature: O. Anweiler, 'Die russische Revolution von 1905', *Jahrbücher für Geschichte Osteuropas* 3 (1955), pp. 161–93; *Die Rätebewegung in Rußland, 1905–1921* (Leiden, 1958); J.H.L. Keep, *The Rise of Social Democracy in Russia* (London, 1963); A. Fischer, *Russische Sozialdemokratie und bewaffneter Aufstand im Jahre 1905* (Wiesbaden, 1967).

Fundamental Laws which followed. Thanks to these, as well as to courts-martial and the army, calm was restored. In the years of political reaction which followed, not all the concessions could be rescinded. The new electoral laws created a workers' curia, a small group of Social Democrats was elected to the Duma, labour unions were legalised as well as a number of labour newspapers (although they were always threatened by the censor). In addition, some strictly regulated and supervised civil liberties such as freedom of assembly and association were introduced. This could not, however, remove the danger that the working class would again prove an abundant source of recruits for mass revolutionary movements. Although the freedoms granted to workers were limited, the fact that they were conceded at all might have prompted some groups to adopt an attitude similar to that of the reformist wing of West European labour organisations which had abandoned revolution and now hoped to reform the system. However, the Russian regime always managed in the end to sap any confidence that the existing order could be perfected.[23]

While Wilhelm II occasionally liked to speak of turning his guns on the Reds, Nicholas actually engaged in the practice. The police triggered a terrible bloodbath at a labour demonstration in the Lena Goldfields in April 1912 and again at the Putilov works in Petersburg in July 1914. The nervousness and brutality of the authorities derived from the fact that the Russian proletariat was still a wellspring of discontent and protest. During the two years before the First World War the economic cycle in Russian industry prompted another wave of strikes which were repeatedly transformed into political demonstrations under socialist watchwords, especially in the two capital cities. When Poincaré paid a state visit to Petersburg in July 1914, he was confronted by a general strike involving approximately 200,000 workers. Not only Soviet researchers but also Americans speak quite properly of a revolutionary situation which did not abate until war erupted.[24]

The period before the First World War illustrated time and again a fact which had first become evident in 1905: whenever the Autocracy was on the verge of being toppled, the working class would

23. The history of Russian Social Democracy between 1905 and 1917 has not yet been adequately covered. For the trade unions see W. Grinewitsch, *Die Gewerkschaftsbewegung in Rußland*, vol.1, 1905–1914 (Berlin, 1927).
24. L.H. Haimson, 'The Problem of Social Stability in Urban Russia', *Slavic Review* XXIII (1964), pp. 619–42; XXIV (1965), pp. 1–56.

play an important role in determining the outcome. Unlike the peasant masses, the working class represented an organised force, or at least one capable of organisation and coordination. Furthermore, it was concentrated in the most important cities of the Empire, in localities which were centres of both power and political interest. There is no denying that the mentality and attitudes of the proletariat constituted a menace to the established authorities. Anyone who succeeded in mobilising the working class in a moment of crisis could quickly bring the old regime to the brink of catastrophe.

As we have seen, rural society had been ravaged and conditions were desperate. Abject poverty was widespread among the peasantry and broad groupings within the population vented their misery and despair in upheaval and elemental revolt. In the cities, the workers were prepared to resist and had shown that their movement could easily spawn gigantic political demonstrations. In the light of both these factors, the continuing ability of the old regime to cling to power seems quite remarkable. Despite losing wide public support, it overcame the danger of revolution for decades on end. The resilience which the political system displayed, despite all its weakness and fragility, needs to be investigated. This leads from the *social* preconditions of the revolution to the *political* situation.

3

Political Preconditions of the Revolution

Anyone examining the dynamics of social change and economic development in Russia must find it remarkable that the Autocracy could survive as late as 1917 without great damage and that a catastrophic war was needed to destroy it. The old regime demonstrated remarkable tenacity even on the verge of disaster, and its resilience seemed to disprove all those who had been predicting the end of tsarism for generations. Even the centrifugal forces generated by the multinational composition of the Empire had been controlled. The government was certainly very concerned about demands for national equality and autonomy, especially during the uprisings of 1905–6, but such demands never threatened the actual existence of the Empire. Even the particularly thorny Polish problem had been handled satisfactorily. Historians often overlook the fact that nationalist movements in Russia contributed very little to the final collapse of the state, unlike the case in Austria–Hungary. This too can be seen as a consequence of Russia's underdevelopment.[1] The explosive power of nationalism, so apparent in 1917, was a result of the revolution, not one of the causes.

Historians are always inclined to focus on signs of dissolution and crisis during a pre-revolutionary period. However, if one fails to appreciate the old regime's political power and resilience, important preconditions of the revolution will be obscured and the revolution itself as well as fundamental questions belonging to the year 1917 will not appear in the proper light. Paramount among these

1. For the state of the research see the exemplary study of R. Pipes, *The Formation of the Soviet Union. Communism and Nationalism 1917–1923*, 2nd revised edn. (Cambridge, Mass., 1964) as well as H. Seton-Watson, *The Russian Empire, 1801–1917* (Oxford, 1967); G. v. Rauch, *Rußland — Staatliche Einheit und nationale Vielfalt* (Munich, 1953).

questions is why, after the collapse of the monarchy, other political alternatives besides the Bolshevik Soviet State did not seem credible — why, in other words, parliamentary democracy did not flourish in Russia. An investigation into the political situation in autocratic Russia should therefore shed light on the problems faced by its opponents. We shall have to enquire whether the relative stability of tsarism was not due in part to the weakness of its potential political heirs.

Although the old social order had clearly been decaying ever since the 1860s, the government bureaucracy on which the Auto-cracy rested had not suffered a similar decline. While the traditional agrarian order crumbled, the bureaucracy most certainly did not. In the West, the difficult process of social change had been fuelled by and large by forces already existing within society. In Russia, however, state initiatives provided most of the impetus and this necessarily fostered rapid growth in state responsibilities. Civil emancipation of the peasantry and abolition of the nobility's con-trol over the land multiplied the number of administrative problems which the government had to handle. At the same time, the indus-trial revolution invaded many areas of Russian life and demanded complex, novel responses from the government. The many social emergencies and conflicts which arose required repeated interven-tion on the part of the state. As bureaucratic competences and responsibilities mushroomed, Russian bureaucrats gained more power than ever before. Although the history of the last fifty years of the tsarist administration had yet to be written,[2] a comparison with the period before 1860 would certainly show that as govern-ment responsibilities accumulated, methods improved a great deal, the capacity of the administration was stepped up and the quality and efficiency of the bureaucracy improved. Prussian levels of efficiency were probably never attained, but right down to the local districts the Russian *chinovnik* was no longer the corrupt, unedu-cated despot of so many caricatures, no longer the discharged subaltern who suddenly surfaced in public office. Now the bureauc-racy was dominated by educated experts with at least a secondary school certificate and possibly a university diploma.[3]

2. The material includes the excellent survey by E. Amburger, *Geschichte der Behördenorganisation Rußlands von Peter dem Großen bis 1917* (Leiden, 1966). For the administrative machinery before 1914 see G.L. Yaney, 'Some Aspects of the Imperial Russian Government of the Eve of the First World War', *The Slavonic and East European Review* XLIII, no. 100 (December 1964), pp. 68–90.
3. The connection is touched upon by Alf Edeen, 'The Civil Service, its Compos-

These functionaries were quick to react when they perceived any competition. They were resolved above all that the duties and services performed by society at large would not develop into political rights which detracted from their powers or which could even be turned against them. And yet this very kind of challenge to the bureaucracy did begin to emerge in imperial Russia. The activities of the local institutions of self-government created after 1864 posed a particularly vexatious problem. In the provinces and districts, the public was now represented by elected bodies known officially as *zemskie uchrezhdeniya* (rural institutions) — or by the old name of *zemstvo* (the land).[4] A tiered electoral system brought together representatives of the large landowners (mostly aristocrats) and representatives of the peasantry and the urban classes. Sufficient precautions had been taken in drafting the law to ensure that the zemstvos would remain loyal institutions of state operating within the desired limitations, and that they would not develop into a type of provincial government which could unite the public and demand political freedom. The bureaucracy expected the curial franchise of 1890 (which remained in effect until 1917) to afford the requisite loyalty over the long term. Electoral property qualifications guaranteed the wealthy social strata (especially the rural gentry) an absolute majority while freezing the peasants' share at about 10 per cent.

The closely regulated organs of local self-government had been intended to bind the estates and classes of the nation to the bureaucratic state, but in actual fact the zemstvos developed a life of their own. Their duties and areas of competence became a perpetual incentive to seek independence and freedom of action. Important segments of the public administration with clear national significance were entrusted to the zemstvos: much of the provincial economy and transportation system, rural schools, tax collecting and health and social services. In 1900 these institutions, including the urban municipalities, counted more than 50,000 employees — teachers, physicians and engineers who owed their livelihood not to the central state but to local society. The entire national bureaucracy

---

ition and Status', *Transformation of Russian Society*, pp. 274ff.
4. For a contemporary overview see B. Veselovskii, *Istoriya zemstva za sorok let* (History of the Zemstvo (vols. 1–4, St Petersburg, 1909–11); for its political relevance, W. Golubew, 'Das Semstwo' in J. Melnik (ed.), *Russen über Rußland* (Frankfurt, 1906); informative overviews can be found in A. Vucinich, 'The State and Local Community' in *Transformation of Russian Society*, pp. 191–209; J. Walkin, *The Rise of Democracy in Pre-Revolutionary Russia* (London, 1963), pp. 153–82.

with its army of functionaries, judges and clerks was only about twice as large.[5] Nevertheless, the zemstvos still did not succeed between 1864 and 1914 in making many inroads into the central administration or in gaining the balance of power. The reasons can be found in the continuing ability of the old institutions of state to integrate the nation. The organs of local self-government were more an appendix to the national administration than its opponent, or even a full-blown competitor.

The very existence of zemstvos spurred hopes for further liberalisation, but such dreams were frustrated time and again by massive opposition from the bureaucracy. From their inception, the zemstvos had inspired and encouraged liberal tendencies in the rural gentry and professional intelligentsia. Hope spread that local self-government would help to inculcate constitutionalism, a first step in the progressive reform of government and a point of departure for moving Russia in a liberal and even democratic direction. Opposition circles were impressed by the fact that the zemstvos represented *all* classes of the population and could claim to be the legitimate representative of the people in its confrontation with the state. Thus a civic pride was born — though over-confidence and an inability to perceive the limitations were widespread. Since the zemstvos included all strata of the population, the idea soon arose of extending self-government beyond the provincial level and of crowning the system with an all-Russian *zemskii sobor*, a national assembly embodying an essentially Russian form of representation. Such a concept reawakened old dreams: an active zemstvo-parliament endowed with solid institutional foundations in the provinces and districts and with well-defined spheres of competence beyond the reach of the state bureaucracy could stimulate further developments, perhaps a gradual transformation of the Autocracy into a constitutional monarchy. Not only the German model but even the more liberal British one was thought to be both desirable and attainable in Russia.

So-called zemsvto liberals wanted to see self-government extended not only upward towards the pinnacle of power but downward into the rural districts. Beneath the district level, the power of the land captains, the *zemskie nachalniki*, would be revoked and the peasant communes would be opened to people of other classes.

5. See the statistics in L.K. Erman, *Intelligentsiya v pervoi russkoi revolyutsii* (The intelligentsia in the first Russian Revolution) (Moscow, 1966), pp. 7ff.

Behind all this was the expectation that the social composition of the zemstvos could be thoroughly modernised, primarily by re-forming the electoral laws to allow for more equal representation of the various social classes. Even if the extent of such 'democratisation' had remained limited, these self-governing bodies would certainly have accumulated authority. Every extension of their social base was likely to force the bureaucratic, authoritarian state gradually to change its posture. Such hopes were therefore not entirely groundless, and at the time of the Russo-Japanese War the zemstvos seemed to be slowly driving the old regime in this direction.[6] However, the state bureaucracy stiffened its resolve after the turmoil of 1905 and 1906 and rapidly recovered its strength. The zemstvos became entrapped in a pseudo-constitutional system based not on democratic urges but on the reaction of the 1890s. The bureaucracy lost none of its power, while the zemstvos remained politically impotent with only limited responsibilities. When the Revolution erupted in the spring of 1917, the zemstvos had very little chance of resisting pressure from the revolutionary soviets and of establishing themselves in the minds of the people as the cornerstone of democratic self-government.

The tenacity of the old regime should by no means be ascribed to brute force alone, as if the government was only held together by loyal Cossacks or skilful police agents. The balance of forces that kept the Autocracy in power for so long did not depend solely on the bayonets of privileged praetorian guards or on the state's ability to uncover political conspiracies and hang or banish the traitors to Siberia. Much more important was the strong magnetic attraction which the old regime still held over much of the population until its final collapse. Although many groups of industrial workers were disaffected, the government could still count by and large on the loyalty of the peasants, who considered the Autocracy to be elevated above all earthly interference. Whenever peasant disturbances erupted, the crowds directed abuse not at the Tsar but at others whom they held responsible for misery and injustice: major landowners and their stewards, petty officials, tax collectors, usurers, bloodsuckers and Jews, who, it was said, had nailed the son of God to the cross. Deeply ingrained patriotism, reinforced by the Russian Orthodox religion, served again and again to check anarchistic

6. I.P. Belokonskii, *Zemskoe dvizhenie* (The Zemstvo Movement), 2nd edn. (Moscow, 1914).

impulses. Loyalty to the state was weak, but love of country substituted admirably and created a place for the Tsar in the peasants' view of the world.[7] True, the convulsive disintegration of the traditional agrarian order had shown that the spiritual foundations of the Autocracy were in danger of evaporating in many areas. However, the loyalty of the simple, uneducated people remained firm even in the midst of the First World War. Peasants composed the largest class in the Russian army and they proved extremely unreceptive to attempts at revolutionary agitation before the spring of 1917.

It is important to realise that this situation severely constrained opposition and revolutionary politics in Russia. Neither liberal nor socialist groups ever penetrated the great mass of the peasant population. Even though skilfully planned propaganda reached the villages during times of general unrest, none of the political parties was able to establish a permanent base of support. The countryside, where 80 per cent of the population lived, was for the most part disinterested in politics. According to official statistics compiled around the turn of the century, the illiteracy rate among the adult population stood at 76 per cent. The social classes which did provide fertile ground for political agitation in pre-revolutionary Russia were virtually identical with the educated classes. If political beliefs and ideas were to spread further, part of the working class would have to be politicised. This task too fell to the intelligentsia.

According to the census of 1897 only a little more than *1 per cent* of the population benefitted from an education beyond the three or four grades of elementary school. In the entire Empire some 130,000 people claimed to be college or university graduates. Statistics were also gathered on what could be called white-collar workers in middle-class professions.[8] They numbered fewer than three-quarters of a million, including officers, functionaries, railway employees and midwives. If one wished to use these statistics to compose a 'bourgeoisie' in the Western sense, a roughly equivalent figure could be used. Members of the 'liberal professions' seemed especially prone to adopt political positions. This was an extremely small but growing caste: in 1897 about 15,000 doctors and dentists, not quite 10,000 lawyers and notaries, approximately 6,000 engin-

7. M. Cherniavsky, *Tsar and People: Studies in Russian Myths* (New Haven, Conn., 1961).
8. Employment statistics according to L.K. Erman (cf. n.5); see also H. Seton-Watson, *The Russian Empire, 1801–1917* (Oxford, 1967), pp. 534ff.

eers and technicians in industry and agriculture and approximately 3,300 people who described themselves as writers or academics. More numerous was the army of poorly paid teachers who could have organised to promote their own political goals. About 160,000 school teachers and private tutors were registered, although by 1906 fewer than one-tenth of them had joined together in the Union of Russian Teachers. These figures indicate how slender the potential foundations of political activity still were.

Besides these quantifiable conditions were qualitative factors which perhaps had an even greater impact on political organisations. The parties in Russia were relatively new, but the virtual confinement of their activities to the educated classes lent them a strangely antiquated air.[9] The modern type of party representing a particular interest group failed to develop. Capitalists, entrepreneurs and industrialists did not organise as a political faction; instead, their associations dealt directly with the government. Despite many complaints, they found that this provided adequate protection for their interests in official policy-making. Those individuals who harboured further political ambitions sought support among liberals or at times even among the revolutionaries. The nobility during the pre-revolutionary period also lacked representation by a political party which supported its particular interests. One reason for this is very apparent; the Russian aristocracy no longer had common interests which could be adequately defined. Those who did try to articulate these interests received little support — as did every conservative ideology of the time. The social transformation underway ever since the emancipation of the serfs had liquidated the Russian nobility as a social class and done more to bring about the economic ruin of the landed aristocracy than any previous event. By the time of the First World War, the rural gentry had been absorbed for the most part into the strata of private landowners whose political beliefs lacked a strong thrust of their own. Many of these landowners thought at least privately along liberal lines. From an economic point of view, however, the landowners supported protectionism and hoped to persuade the government to concern itself with the problems of the rural estates rather than with industrial

9. For the conditions under which the parties developed as a political problem see K.v. Beyme, *Politische Soziologie im zaristischen Rußland* (Wiesbaden, 1965). For lengthy, older self-descriptions from a Marxist or left-liberal point of view: *Obshchestvennoe dvizhenie v Rossii v nachale XX v.* (The Social Movement in Russia at the beginning of the twentieth century) (vols. 1–4, St Petersburg, 1909–12).

development. At the same time, the major landowners clung ten-
aciously to the political status quo because only the hated regime
could protect them against the imminent threat of peasant land
hunger. It was therefore only natural after 1905 for many of the
more substantial landowners to throw their support behind the
'Octobrists', a party which was satisfied with the pseudo-constitutionalism of the period.[10]

The ambivalance of these various interest groups rendered political organisation difficult. This was especially true of the fractured
liberal grouping which gave birth in 1905 to the most important
opposition party of the pre-revolutionary period, the Constitutional Democrats (*kadety*). Of all the political groupings, this one
most resembled a western-style bourgeois party. The Kadets received support from the professional intelligentsia composed of
lawyers, doctors, professors and teachers. However, no solid
middle class existed to widen this political base. As a result, the
developing party did not represent a common interest but a very
loose collection of similar attitudes. It was bound together by a
handful of modern principles, such as the desire to see Russia
overcome its political and social backwardness, to draw closer to a
constitutional monarchy on English lines and to guarantee political
freedoms. The Kadet notion of freedom also extended to cultural
matters and the party believed that public enlightenment and education in the broadest sense were necessary if Russia was to gain a
respected place in the company of modern nations.[11]

The liberals sought support in the zemstvos and among the
landed gentry. However, interaction with these groups, closely
allied to the regime in many ways, diminished the party's vigour.
Instead of seeking 'political liberation', the Kadets were often

10. Cf. L.H. Haimson, 'The Parties and the State' in *Transformation of Russian Society*, pp. 110–45; H. Jablonowski, 'Die russischen Rechtsparteien 1905–1917' in *Rußlandstudien. Gedenkschrift für O. Hoetzsch* (Stuttgart, 1957), pp. 43–55; H. Rogger, 'The Formation of the Russian Right', *California Slavic Studies* III (1964), pp. 66–94; also the studies by the same author in *Journal of Modern History* XXXVI (1964), pp. 398–415, *Slavic Review* XXV (1966), pp. 615–29. There is no satisfactory monograph on the parties during the pseudo-constitutional period; for the period from 1881 to 1904 see the broad survey by Valdo Zilli, *La Rivoluzione Russa 1905. La Formazione dei Partiti Politici* (Naples, 1963). Still noteworthy is A. Levin, *The Second Duma. A Study of the Social-Democratic Party and the Russian Constitutional Experiment* (Yale University Press, 1940; repr. 1966).
11. See the literature mentioned in chapter 2, n.12 as well as M. Karpovich, 'Two Types of Russian Liberalism: Maklakov and Miliukov' in J. Simmons (ed.), *Continuity and Change in Russian and Soviet Thought* (Cambridge, Mass., 1955), pp. 129–43.

forced into opportunistic compromises with the old order. Expansion of the party base in this direction meant that liberal protest was tempered and rebelliousness muffled by medals and smart uniforms. The Kadets even felt some compunction about demands for universal and equal suffrage because they feared that their goal of well-ordered parliamentarism would be quickly overwhelmed by the anarchic despotism of the masses. More radical sectors of the liberal intelligentsia attempted repeatedly to win support from the left and took measures to include revolutionary socialists in the great national 'liberation movement' against tsarism. However, this approach produced neither a secure position nor an encouraging response from the people. The highly respectable proponents of constitutional democracy found it impossible to join forces with those who raised the spectre of violence and armed resistance. The Kadets feared that their watered-down republicanism, not to mention their liberalism, could only suffer from an alliance such as this. The wave of support which buoyed them up for a short period during 1905–06 seemed to promise a leading role, but mere passionate appeals and noble, even courageous demonstrations of their own desire for freedom were not sufficient to take advantage of the situation. The regime succeeded once again in consolidating itself without having to pay the price of parliamentary government. By the time of Stolypin's *coup d'état* of June 1907, which eventually resulted in the unmanageable second Duma being replaced with a pliant, loyal successor, the liberal opposition had become incapable of generating policies inimical to the Autocracy.

Through all of this, the Kadets never learned to view themselves as a party representing just one segment of society. Their appeals were always directed to society at large, to all classes and social strata. The clearer it became that they could not win the political support of the nation, the more they were inclined to escape into the nationalism fostered by the great power policies of the government. Pride in Russia's might would compensate for the failure of liberal policies and social and cultural programmes.[12] The Kadets grew determined that their patriotism would not be outshone by that of the government, and foreign affairs provided a strong basis for a consensus between themselves and the regime. When individual

12. J. Jablonowski, 'Die Stellungnahme der russischen Parteien zur Außenpolitik der Regierung von der englisch-russischen Verständigung bis zum Ersten Weltkriege', *Forschungen zur osteuropäischen Geschichte* V (1957), pp. 60–92.

Kadets occasionally chose to speak out eloquently or even caustically in the Duma about the foolishness or dangerousness of official foreign policy, it was not because they wished to see things done differently — only better. During the First World War the Kadets re-established themselves as a corrosive force in the autocratic system. However, they failed to renounce the war aims of the government and were destroyed when they dared to transfer these goals to the Revolution of 1917. Russian liberalism finally floundered on the noble illusion that it spoke for the nation, on suggestive fictions which had prospered only because the liberals were so isolated from the rest of society.

The revolutionary camp, especially the Socialist Revolutionaries, suffered from similar disappointments.[13] This party of the intelligentsia never overcame the discrepancy between reality and the goals which it set for itself. Its programme endeavoured first and foremost to assist the peasantry, but there were no actual peasants in its ranks save a few, pampered specimens. The agrarian socialism of the party was the brainchild of professional revolutionaries who added Marxism to the venerable intellectual heritage of the populist movement and produced a bizarre mixture. The intellectual party which resulted was fired by a revolutionary fervour which could be shared alike by obscure village schoolmasters and debating circles of radical students, literate workers and army officers. One should not fail to include either those esoteric circles which were prepared to sacrifice their own lives because they believed that hurling bombs into ministerial carriages would precipitate mass revolution or because they wished to demonstrate by means of revolutionary terror that an elite of Russian youths were prepared to offer their lives in order to purge the sins of their fathers and cultivated society alike. As with the Kadets, the Socialist Revolutionaries rejected inferences that they represented only a part of the population or just *one* class. They insisted that they spoke on behalf of all labouring Russians, a people which had not yet been divided along class lines and which lived in its villages and factories as one indivisible, indestructible organism. This people allegedly suffered from the same lack of freedom, the same exploitation and the same sufferings,

---

13. O.H. Radkey, *The Agrarian Foes of Bolshevism. omise and Default of the Russian Socialist Revolutionaries 1917* (New York, 1958). The authoritative history of the prewar Socialist Revolutionary Party is by M. Hildermeier, *Die Sozialrevolutionäre Partei Russlands. Agrassozialismus und Modernisierung im Zarenreich* (1900–1914) (Cologne–Vienna, 1978).

and it demanded the same future: socialisation of property, abolition of the division of labour and freedom within a social order composed of a federated series of small units and of an association of all working people whether urban or rural. The plans were grandiose but they ran counter to the times. When the peasantry finally did turn to the SRs in 1917 this party of intellectuals failed, in its political dilettantism, to abide by its own programme. The Revolution quickly blew it aside.

The Social Democratic party came closest to being a modern party representing a particular political interest, but even it could never quite bridge the gap between the intelligentsia and the class it wished to reach. Its claim to be the party of the proletariat was better founded in theory than in practice. Social Democrats still viewed their role largely in terms of their traditional belief in a dialectical bond between the intelligentsia and the working class — a class which was not yet quite aware of the bond's existence. This was not the only problem. The party's self-image was damaged to an even larger extent by the difficulties it experienced with Russian society as a whole. Even if the proletariat could be mobilised for revolution it would not cease being a minority. The dictatorship of the Russian proletariat would not result, as Marx had indicated, in the dictatorship of the vast majority. On the contrary, if class rule by the proletariat was ever to occur in its pure form it would have to be directed against the majority of the population, for the mass of Russian peasantry were small landholders whose outlook in Marxist terms was considered to be more bourgeois than proletarian, despite their poverty. The more democratic elements within the Social Democratic Party recoiled at this prospect because this party too claimed to speak on behalf of *all* working people who suffered and were exploited. The party's own intellectual analysis thus presented them with a dilemma.[14]

Some comfort could be taken from the conviction that the proletarian revolution in Russia was still years away. For Russia had still of course to pass through the 'bourgeois' revolution — through 1848 so to speak. The Social Democrats would first have to ensure that the collapse of tsarism engendered a bourgeois revolution and the establishment of a democratic republic similar to the at least

14. For this see D. Geyer, *Lenin in der russischen Sozialdemokratie* (Cologne, 1962) and 'Die russische Sozialdemokratie als parteigeschichtliches Problem' in *Geschichte und Gegenwartsbewußtsein. Festschrift für H. Rothfels* (Göttingen, 1963), pp. 106–21.

tolerable regime which arose in France after the Paris Commune. However, any admission that the existence of Social Democratic party was untimely did nothing to further practical decisions. Who in Russia would conduct the bourgeois revolution? The Russian bourgeoisie was evidently still very weak. Among the confined circles of the leading industrialists where it had some strength, the bourgeoisie clung to the very regime which the laws of history dictated it should be trying to overthrow. The tiny liberal-democratic faction could hardly engineer a successful revolt against tsarism with only the support of the professional intelligentsia. As a result of this dilemma, the Russian Social Democrats were unsure of their own identity and in their politics largely exhausted themselves in ruinous factional strife and intellectual controversy. The Mensheviks (the faction most loyal to the Marxist orthodoxy of the large sister party in Germany) experimented after 1905 with socio-political reformism, even though this entailed the risk of being co-opted by their own class enemies.[15] For the rest they practised patience, confident that the future belonged to them. The international revolution and the grand collapse of bourgeois societies in the West could not fail to topple the old regime in Russia.

Lenin alone drew decisive and positive consequences from the minority position which the Russian revolutionaries found themselves in. The Bolsheviks strove not to achieve a democratic consensus within the working class or the labouring masses in general but to position themselves to seize power for their party cadres when the revolution occurred. Lenin concerned himself with the organisation and operations of the party and with the positions it needed to adopt in order to achieve what the vanguard of the revolution considered necessary because it was right. Confidence that the party could 'make things happen' (H. Freyer) required an apparatus and functionaries able to steer and oversee developments. However, when the First World War broke out, Lenin's revolutionary policies had still not developed beyond the level of theoretical projections.

Anyone who wishes to understand the political situation in pre-revolutionary Russia must fully appreciate the underdevelop-

---

15. Further studies on Menshevik history can be expected from the group working under L. Haimson. See meanwhile S.M. Schwarz, *The Russian Revolution of 1905. The Workers' Movement and the Formation of Bolshevism and Menshevism* (Chicago, 1967). For relations with German Social Democracy see the article by the present author in *Internal Review of Social History* 3 (1958), pp. 195–219 and 418–44, as well as Peter Lösche's recent study: *Der Bolschewismus im Urteil der deutschen Sozialdemokratie, 1903–1920* (Berlin, 1967).

ment of political parties. With no politicised society to contend with, the old regime could create the relative stability it needed in order to survive the process of social transformation without having to accept any changes in the political structure that would have appreciably affected the Autocracy and its bureaucratic rule. Nascent political parties were easily subdued by police methods or else co-opted in to the pseudo-parliamentarism of the Duma. The fragmented educated class was insisting on the right to form political associations but it still did not represent much more than itself. The intellectuals liked to imagine themselves as the people's representatives but this was a self-appointed role. When tsarism finally collapsed, a host of political alternatives had been worked out and were ready to be put into practise. However, the grandiose designs of these isolated groupings were quickly torn to shreds by the new realities. Both policies and politicians were incapable of standing the strains of a society in the throes of revolution.

4

War and Revolution

The Russian Revolution cannot be imagined without war. War and revolution joined forces in 1905 and their impact was redoubled when tsarist Russia finally crumbled in 1917. There is every reason to say therefore that 'the Revolution was born of the war'.[1] Birth, however, should not be confused with its causes. As we have seen, the Revolution began its gestation long before the First World War. While war was a certainly an immediate cause of the 1917 Revolution, it also had a far more extensive impact. Long before the conflict erupted and transformed Russia and the entire world, the hopes of revolutionary thinkers and activists had been stimulated by the very existence of war as a historical phenomenon.

War and revolution obviously do not always move in tandem, but they can do so as the ancient term 'civil war' indicates. War did not reach its full potential as a stimulus of revolution and revolution as a stimulus of war until both had been 'democratised', i.e. until the transition from traditional cabinet wars into wars waged by entire nations had modernised warfare, and until mass social movements had effected structural change in revolutions. The new situation can be expressed by the terms 'war of revolution' and 'revolutionary war'. Wars become revolutionary when they aim not only to capture the enemy's territory but also to overthrow his political and social system, that is, when not only states are transformed but entire social systems. This phenomenon could be observed outside France after 1793. The struggles which followed, especially those against Napoleon, provided further examples. Even the enemies of the Revolution — the forces of counter-revolution, of legitimacy and finally of restoration — adopted the new, revolutionary principle of warfare. The standards which classical international law had

---

1. E. Hölzle, *Lenin 1917. Die Geburt der Revolution aus dem Kriege* (Munich, 1957).

developed to distinguish *justified* from *unjustified* wars were thus
invalidated. Ever since, modern revolutionary thought has never
fully divorced itself from the phenomenon of war.

The importance of this new understanding of war quickly becomes apparent if the history of Marxism and the socialist movement is considered. For Marx, every war against tsarism and
Russian despotism was necessarily progressive and imbued with
revolutionary potential — witness his Russophobia and sympathy
for Poland. To be opposed to the bulwark of reaction in Europe
required no further justication.[2] The democratic left in Germany
both during and after 1848 took a very similar view, as did many
liberals. These attitudes survived the passage of time and still
reverberated in 1891 in a speech delivered by August Bebel before
the Erfurt Conference of the German Social Democrats:

> If Russia, the stronghold of cruelty and barbarism, the enemy of all
> human culture, should attack Germany . . . we are just as concerned, nay
> more concerned, than those who hold power. We shall resist. . . . so that
> Germany, that means we ourselves, might be saved and our land freed
> from the barbarians.[3]

The startling new notion that one was defending one's motherland,
originating with the '*levée en masse*' of the French Revolution, was
transmitted from generation to generation, together with Marxist
hostility to Russia. Since Marx and Engels viewed the German
Social Democratic Party as the key to revolution in Europe, the
German Reich was to be defended against Russia — and, as Engels
emphasised, against the French Republic which had taken Russia's
side after 1891:

> If Germany is attacked from east and west, then every means of defence
> is justified. It is a question of national survival and, so far as we are
> concerned, of defending the position and the future opportunities we
> have struggled to achieve. The more revolutionary the war, the more it
> serves our cause . . . [And even more clearly:] . . . If we triumph, our

---

2. For a detailed description of attitudes towards Russia, see H. Krause, *Marx und Engels und das zeitgenössische Rußland* (Gießen, 1958).
3. *Protokoll über die Verhandlungen des Parteitages der Sozialdemokratischen Partei Deutschlands. Abgehalten zu Erfurt vom 14. bis 20. Oktober 1891* (Berlin, 1891), p. 285. See also Bebel's speeches before the German Reichstag on 7 March and 10 December 1904 in *Stenographische Berichte über die Verhandlungen des Reichstags* XI. Legislaturperiode. I. Session, 1. Abschn. 1903/04, Bd. 2, 51. Sitzung, pp. 1583C–1592A; I. Session, 2. Abschn. Bd. 5, 109. Sitzung, pp. 3479B–3490A.

party will take power. Germany's victory is also the victory of the revolution.[4]

Without question, a victorious war is understood here as a source of revolution. Twenty-five years later, this confidence that bourgeois rule could not survive a victorious war helped pave the way for the German Social Democrats to march off to war at the Kaiser's side, a 'war of national defence' whose revolutionary properties already escaped the party leadership.

It would be mistaken to conclude from these statements that Marxism ever adopted a positive view of war for the sake of revolution. If anything, attitudes shifted in the opposite direction. This was due to the fine distinctions customarily drawn between wars which were offensive and defensive, justified and unjustified, progressive and reactionary. Around the turn of the century social-ist parties found this line of reasoning less and less compelling as the connection between economics and world affairs emphasised the arrival of a new, imperialist phase of capitalism which undermined the reasoning behind the previous distinctions. In addition, the existence of a revolutionary movement in imperial Russia increased the difficulty of applying Marxist concepts to determine which side was in the right in case of war. In an imperialist age, wars of national defence could not be justified in the name of revolutionary progress. The enemy seemed to be the same on all sides and the tragedy which every major war would visit on the working classes of all countries could no longer be justified by pointing to revolution.

This may explain why war became the danger which the socialist movement most feared during these years of conflict and crisis in imperialist politics. Socialist agitation *against* war increased dra-matically.[5] Congresses of the Socialist International declared peace and international fraternity to be one of the most urgent problems facing the proletariat. Working-class parties became energetic pro-ponents of compromise and the balance of power in Europe. They even advocated international disarmament and no longer insisted

4. Engels to Bebel, 13 October and 29 September 1891 in F. Engels, *Briefe an Bebel* (Berlin, 1958), pp. 190f., 184.
5. For an excellent summary, introducing new sources and documents, see G. Haupt, *Le congrès manqué. L'international à la veille de la première guerre mondiale* (Paris, 1965); also M.M. Drachkovitch, *Les socialismes français et allemand et le problème de la guerre, 1870–1914* (Geneva, 1953). The pertinent resolutions of the International can be found in J. Kuczynski, *Der Ausbruch des ersten Weltkrieges und die deutsche Sozialdemokratie. Chronik und Analyse* (Berlin, 1957), pp. 174ff.

that disarmament would only be possible after the revolution.[6] /
Underlying these activities was a conviction that a modern war /
between nations was highly detrimental to proletarian class-war and
therefore to revolution and socialism. Memories of earlier links
between war and revolution faded and barely survived in the form
of ritual slogans. Thus the left-wing groups gathered around Rosa
Luxemburg (to which war was a 'fateful consequence of capitalist
development') experienced great difficulty in 1907 when they
wished the Stuttgart anti-war resolution of the Socialist International to include a reference not only to militant pacifism and
anti-militarism but also to their belief that any war whose outbreak
could not be prevented should be exploited in order to hasten the
collapse of class rule.[7]

Russian socialist parties of course shared in the changing attitude
towards war. However, they did not entertain as many doubts as
their Western brothers about the capacity of war to serve the cause
of revolution, especially in view of the impact which war had had on
Russia. Russian socialists and many others had expected that the
Russo-Japanese War would set in motion the destruction of tsarism
and the events of 1905 seemed at first to confirm these hopes.[8]
Despite the rapid defeat of the revolutionary movement, the left
remained covinced that the old regime risked self-destruction if it
dared go to war. Russian socialists therefore adopted an extremely
ambivalent attitude towards war: they could not deny that war
created an opportunity for revolution, but they certainly did not
applaud war on the theory that any armed conflict would necessarily further revolution and the collapse of the tsarist regime.
Socialist pacifism was well developed in Russia as well as in Europe
and the idea of fighting to defend the motherland would have
seemed absurd to Russian revolutionaries before 1914. Typical of
this attitude was the refusal of most socialist groups to favour one
side or the other in the Russo-Japanese War. They supported peace,
not one of the warring parties. It was peace that was in the interests
of the proletariat — whether Russian or Japanese.

6. Cf. Ursula Ratz. 'Karl Kautsky und die Abrüstungskontroverse in der deutschen Sozialdemokratie 1911/12', *International Review of Social History* XI (1966),
pp. 197–227.
7. *Internationaler Sozialisten-Kongreß zu Stuttgart, 18. bis 24. August 1907* (Berlin, 1907), pp. 102. The amendment proposed by R. Luxemburg was supported by
Lenin and his Menshevik opponent Martov.
8. A. Fischer, *Russische Sozialdemokratie und bewaffneter Aufstand im Jahre
1905* (Wiesbaden, 1967), pp. 29ff.

Not all socialists of course adhered to this point of view. Lenin, most notably, had already adopted a different position in 1905. He never shared the pacifist anti-militarism of the Socialist International and stubbornly insisted that the revolutionary quality of a war should be the sole criterion employed by a socialist in judging it. Consequently, some of Lenin's statements about the war in the Far East sounded astonishing and were unparalleled in the extremes to which they went. Unlike his comrades in Russia and the west, Lenin openly supported a Japanese victory. He even declared that 'the struggle of the Russian and international proletariats for socialism' depended to a large extent on the defeat of Russsian absolutism in this war. According to Lenin, the Japanese bourgeoisie was engaged in a progressive struggle against Russian tsarism. Progressive Asia (in the form of Japan) was dealing backward, reactionary Europe (represented by tsarism) a decisive blow, and this 'historic war' therefore had a 'huge revolutionary role' to play. The party should strive to take advantage of this situation and eschew 'banal phrases about peace' which did nothing to assist the exploited classes. The proletariat should certainly agitate untiringly against war and never cease to point out that there would always be wars as long as class rule existed. At the present time, however, the main task was to continue the war by revolutionary means: 'The war is not ended yet by far, but every step toward its continuation brings nearer the hour of a great new war, the war of the people against the autocracy, the war of the proletariat for liberty.'[9] Here the familiar Marxist analysis was evidently being taken up again: it was necessary to take sides in the war, the revolutionary function of the war could be clearly stated and pacificism was unacceptable. Lenin's thesis of 1914 — that the imperialist war should be transformed into a civil war against imperialism — had therefore existed long before in embryonic form.

A comparison with Rosa Luxemburg shows how great the gulf was between Lenin and even left-wing groupings within the European socialist movement. In 1904 Luxemburg spoke not about the progressive role of the war in the Far East but about the danger it posed to the entire international proletariat of sooner or later developing into a world war.[10] The vital interests of the proletariat

9. 'The Fall of Port Arthur' (*Vpered* no. 2, 1/14 January 1905) in Lenin, *Collected Works*, vol. 8 (Moscow, 1962), pp. 53ff.
10. R. Luxemburg, 'Krieg' (*Czerwone Sztandar*, February 1904) in *Ausgewählte Reden und Schriften* (Berlin, 1955), vol. 2, p. 184. Luxemburg also hoped of course

were basically incompatible with any war, according to Luxemburg. The Left should therefore support the international solidarity of working people, not one of the belligerent parties. Lenin, on the other hand, felt that any war that might topple world imperialism should be fanned, e.g. wars of oppressed nations which rose up in the name of self-determination against the imperialist rule of a great power (including colonial rebellions or wars against the colonial powers). Lenin therefore ascribed revolutionary properties to every 'war of national liberation'.[11] It was clear that in this regard he was moving further and further from the accepted view of the Socialist International and that his ideas of revolution had long before taken on a peculiar stamp of their own.

Lenin's critique of the Socialist International, dominated at this time by the German Social Democrats, developed along these lines. As early as 1908 he attacked, with more vigour than the German left ever mustered, the 'opportunistic cowardice' of the German sister party — a party which, under Bebel and Vollmar, insisted that it had to defend the fatherland against every attack and every aggressor. According to Lenin, the working class could not be guided in its attitude to wars by whether they were wars of aggression or self-defence: 'Social Democrats may find themselves even in a position to demand offensive wars.'[12] The following statement about the second Balkan crisis (taken from a letter to Maxim Gorky in 1913) should be regarded in the same light: 'A war between Austria and Russia would be very beneficial to the revolution (in all Eastern Europe). However, it is very unlikely that Franz Joseph and Nikolascha will do us this favour.'[13] Lenin was singular among European socialists in holding views such as these.

When World War I finally erupted — surprising most people but not all — it seemed that, far from enhancing opportunities for a revolution and socialism in Europe, it had actually destroyed them

---

that this war would be 'the grave of tsarism and the cradle of political freedom in Russia'.

11. Cf. Lenin's discussion with R. Luxemburg about the right to self-determination (1914) and the possibility of 'wars of national liberation' (1916): *Collected Works*, vol. 20 and vol. 22, pp. 309–12, 331–3. For R. Luxemburg see the biography by P. Nettl. For a fundamental analysis of the context within the history of ideas: P. Kluke, *Selbstbestimmung. Vom Weg einer Idee durch die Geschichte* (Göttingen, 1963), particularly pp. 37ff.

12. 'Bellicose Militarism and the Anti-Militarist Tactics of Social Democracy' (*Proletarii* no. 33, 23 July/5 August 1908) in Lenin, *Collected Works*, vol. 15 (Moscow, 1962), pp. 196, 198.

13. Letter to Gorky (late January 1913) in *Leninskii Sbornik* I (1924), p. 131.

for many years to come. What many thoughtful socialists had always feared and what forceful agitation against war and militarism had succeeded in papering over now became apparent: European socialism was incapable not only of preventing war but also of inoculating working class parties against chauvinism, so that their members would refuse military service in the decisive hour when the governments of Europe summoned their proletariats to defend the flag and the motherland. In a remarkably perspicacious observation in 1911 Karl Kautsky had remarked that if a war broke out which could possibly be portrayed as defensive *'everyone* will become a patriot at first, even the internationally minded. If a few should possess the superhuman courage to resist . . . the government will not have to raise a finger to neutralise them. The furious mob will slay them itself. . . . .'[14] Under the pressures of the day, socialist interpretations of war dwindled in all the participating countries to a level which had seemed impossible before 1914. Only the tiny Social Democratic faction in the Russian Duma, the Bolsheviks and Mensheviks who knew that there was no large party behind them, resisted the wave of chauvinism which now swept over the land putting a halt to the July strikes. The Russian Social Democrats denounced one enemy: imperialism of all stripes. They directed their calls for peace not to governments but to peoples, whom they urged to dictate the peace terms. However, this passionate appeal was swept aside by patriots on all sides who rose to applaud their respective countries.[15]

The war brought a momentous revision of values within the great socialist parties of Europe, the effect of which is hard to exaggerate. Within days international proletarian solidarity had been thoroughly transformed into enthusiastic solidarity with the national middle classes. This was the bitter fruit of a powerful and self-confident emancipatory process which had shown too little concern for outside events. The socialist parties and the working class together demonstrated that they had the same national loyalties as the bourgeoisie. War had, it seemed, eliminated the traditional sense of alienation and paved the way for a dubious reconciliation with the fatherland, which now embraced its former 'unpatriotic children' and sent them off to die. Could European socialism have

14. K. Kautsky, 'Krieg und Frieden. Betrachtungen zur Maifeier', *Die Neue Zeit*, vol. 2, p. 104.
15. For the posture of the Duma fraction see M. Hellmann (ed.), *Die Russische Revolution 1917.* (dtv-dokumente 227/8, Munich, 1964), pp. 53ff.

suffered a more tragic fate than this war between states and peoples?

The outcome is well known: the German Social Democrats explained that their working class was obliged to heed the call to arms in order to extirpate 'frightful and murderous tsarism' and so preserve the freedom and culture of Europe. This was to be accomplished for the good of humanity which was being wilfully suppressed 'by the greed of the capitalist classes in England and France'. Thanks to the class truce, the internal front became an external one and Germans of all classes lined up against the foreign foe. Socialists convinced themselves that in fighting tsarism they were actually helping to achieve one of the traditional goals of the proletarian movement.[16]

Not only the Germans succumbed — socialists on the other side of the trenches also tried to justify *their* class truce and defensive war. The French comrades viewed imperial Germany as a semi-absolutist, quasi-Asiatic land under the Prussian yoke — a nation dominated by *Junkers* and armed to the teeth. Democratic freedoms such as those enjoyed in France had never flowered despite the presence of a powerful Social Democratic Party. France, it was argued, had a duty to resist the Germany of barracks, police and the spiked helmet, a country in which the blind obedience imposed by the army found its reflection in the discipline of the Social Democratic Party. In short, the French socialists regarded Germany in much the same way, *mutatis mutandis*, as the German socialists regarded Russia, and claims that France was defending reason, progress, freedom and culture against barbarism and despotism resembled the claims of the German comrades like two peas in a pod.[17] Even among Russian Marxists and prominent figures like Plekhanov, the father of social democracy in Russia, voices could be heard justifying the war against Germany. According to Plekhanov, the class-conscious Russian proletariat was uniting with its class brothers in France, Belgium and England in order to oppose the 'imperialistic policies of German *Junkers* and the German bour-

16. Abundant material — especially from the press — can be found in the book by J. Kuczynski which was withdrawn from sale in the GDR: *Der Ausbruch des ersten Weltkrieges* (n.5). See also *Die Internationale und der Weltkrieg* 1. Abt. Materialien, collected by C. Grünberg (Leipzig, 1916). Cf. the presentation of this material from the point of view of the East German government in W. Bartel, *Die Linken in der deutschen Sozialdemokratie im Kampf gegen den Militarismus und Krieg* (Berlin, 1958).
17. For the *Union sacrée* see R. Wohl, *French Communism in the Making* (Stanford, 1966), pp. 44ff. For the position of the Italian socialists see H. König, *Lenin und der italienische Sozialismus, 1915–1921* (Cologne, 1967), pp. 13ff.

goisie' and to take up the struggle against German imperialism whose 'most reliable supporters' were now the German Social Democracts. Plekhanov wrote that something had to be done to 'avert the terrible danger that a German victory would pose to the development of democracy in Europe'.[18] A comparison of the arguments on both sides of the trenches reveals the absurdity of socialist attempts to uncover a progressive side to the war.

Not until the excitement of the first few weeks of the conflict had worn off could cooler heads hope to command an audience. Outside the established parties a front of anti-war socialist agitators soon began to form, small groups at first which refused to see the essence of European socialism in an internal truce with the class enemy. These groups tried to reawaken feelings of proletarian class solidarity, despite the slaughter, and heal the damage which the war had inflicted on the Socialist International. The movement was based on the belief that governments would have to be confronted with an overwhelming desire for peace on the part of their own peoples and forced to sign a democratic peace treaty immediately. The search for peace took precedence over all other issues. Radical democratic pacifism was establishing its priorities and there was no interest in calls for revolution.

Only a small minority on the fringe of this so-called 'Zimmerwald movement'[19] drew any more far-reaching conclusions. In addition to denouncing imperialist governments as solely responsible for the devastating loss of life and limb and to decrying the shameful treachery of the majority socialists, this minority attempted to transform the peace movement into a struggle to overthrow capitalist rule by means of an international revolution. Lenin was the most determined proponent of this point of view. He was responsiblle for the appeal not simply to pine for a dubious peace but to take up the 'only real war of liberation', 'to transform the present imperialistic war into a civil war' against imperialism and against 'the bourgeoisie of all nations in order to gain political

18. Cf. G. Tschudnowsky's detailed overview of the attitude to the war of Russian socialist groups in C. Grünberg, *Archiv für die Geschichte des Sozialismus und der Arbeiterbewegung* VI (1916), pp. 60–94, IX (1921), pp. 356–412.
19. For the Zimmerwald movement see A. Balabanoff, *Die Zimmerwalder Bewegung 1914 bis 1918* (Leipzig, 1928); A. Rosmer, *Le mouvement ouvrier pendant la guerre. De l'union sacrée à Zimmerwald* (Paris, 1936); M. Fainsod, *International Socialism and the World War* (Cambridge, Mass., 1935); O.H. Gankin, H.H. Fisher, *The Bolsheviks and the World War. The Origins of the Third International* (Stanford, 1940). Cf. the analysis of the East German historian A Reisberg, *Lenin und die Zimmerwalder Bewegung* (Berlin, 1966).

power and victory for socialism'. The working class of every warring nation had the duty to help defeat its *own* government.[20]

As we have already seen, long before 1914, Lenin had expressed the view that war could further the cause of revolution. Now that the entire imperialist system was engaged in a great war, he adapted his revolutionary thinking to the monumental scale of world events. World war should end in world revolution, a radical about-face not only in Europe but around the globe. This theory of international civil war obviously burst the bounds of conventional European Marxism. Th new goals which Lenin proposed immediately raised the question of the forces that could be mobilised to support them. These forces certainly did not include the parties of the old, prewar International. Lenin declared the Second International dead, destroyed for ever by the unfathomable treachery of its leaders,[21] and he demanded a clear, irrevocable break with all those who had gone over to the enemies of the proletariat. Among such traitors Lenin numbered not only supporters of the class truce (whom he called 'social chauvinists'), but also groupings within the socialist parties, such as the Zimmerwald movement, which opposed the war but strove for a democratic peace rather than for civil war. Lenin believed that these 'social pacifists' and 'centrists', as he called them, exhibited the same dangerous opportunism which had been largely responsible for the collapse of the old International.

What Lenin demanded was nothing less than the abandonment of all parties and organisations belonging to the prewar socialist movement and the creation of fundamentally different, revolutionary International. This third, 'Communist' International would unite those who remained loyal to the cause of revolutionary socialism.[22] Lenin's definition of loyalty was so severe, however, that there could be no meeting of organised forces, only the almost complete isolation in which the exiled Bolshevik leader now found himself with his programme for civil war.

Lenin was intent not on purging the existing socialist parties but on creating a new revolutionary organisation deeply antagonistic to the old parties. The great revolution which Lenin had in mind

20. Lenin's (and Zinoviev's) essays from the war years were first collected in N. Lenin and G. Sinowjew, *Gegen den Strom* (Verlag der Kommunistischen Internationale, 1921).

21. Cf. 'The Position and Tasks of the Socialist International' (*Sotsial-Demokrat* no. 33, 1 December 1914) in Lenin, *Collected Works*, vol. 21 (Moscow, 1962), pp. 35–41.

22. For Lenin's demands for a 'Third International' see ibid.

would draw its strength from other sources. Those who wished to remain socialists would have to go 'down lower and deeper to the real masses', to that twisted, tormented and stifled proletariat and quasi-proletariat which, unlike those who were participating in the profits of the bourgeoisie, still made up the vast majority. Here were to be found the teeming millions which the party could weld into a mass revolutionary movement. Beyond Europe, Lenin found another abundant source of recruits for the revolution against imperialism, a source whose revolutionary potential he had realised before 1914; namely, the peoples inhabiting the exploited regions of the imperialist system, the colonies and semi-colonies of the 'civilised world'. The imperialist countries had become such a parasite on some 100 million 'uncivilised' people that even part of the working class, the so-called 'labour aristocracy', had been bribed by the bourgeoisie into participating in the profits squeezed from the sweat of these peoples. 'Up to 1,000 million people, i.e. over half the entire population of the earth' lived in these zones of imperialist exploitation, according to Lenin.[23] These masses had to be prodded into action. In order for the colonies successfully to wage 'progressive and revolutionary' war against the colonial powers, certain criteria would have to be met: either enormous numbers of people in major oppressed countries like China or India would have to engage in a united effort or, preferably, wars of national liberation in the colonies would coincide with proletarian revolutions in the imperialist countries.

In this revolutionary scenario, exploited and oppressed peoples around the world would rise as one against imperialism and those who benefitted from it. This resembles the Maoist perspective: the revolution of the poor, of the tormented of this world against leeches and parasites. In theory at least, a powerful front was created, a reserve army for world revolution, consisting of the colonised and semi-colonised peoples of Asia and the Orient, the masses of workers and peasants in Eastern Europe, the oppressed peoples and nationalities of Russia, Austria-Hungary and Ottoman Turkey and the proletarian classes of Europe, which had been betrayed by bourgeois influence within labour unions and parties. Revolutionary eruptions would originate in these great hotbeds of

---

23. 'Imperialism and the Split in Socialism' (October 1916) in Lenin, *Collected Works*, vol. 23 (New York, 1962), pp. 105–20. For Lenin's theory of imperialism, see 'Imperialism, the Highest Stage of Capitalism' (1916, published 1917) in *Collected Works*, vol. 22 (New York, 1962), pp. 185–304.

revolt — a socialist, proletarian revolution in the West, a democratic revolution in the agrarian East, revolutionary wars of national liberation among the oppressed peoples inside and outside Europe, and revolt in the colonial world.

In the course of the years 1915 and 1916, Lenin continually pondered the question of how this world revolution could be ignited. He laid particular emphasis on the opportunities which existed in Russia and believed that the European proletariat would not necessarily take the lead. If the revolution stagnated in the West, Eastern Europe and Asia could initiate developments once tsarism had been militarily defeated. The defeat of tsarism might therefore serve as the initial spark. Imperialism would be struck at its 'weakest link' because this 'most barbarian and reactionary of all goverments' continued to hold the greatest number of nations and populations under its yoke. When some Russian comrades asked Lenin what he intended to do if his party were swept to power by the war, he answered:

> We would propose peace to *all* the belligerents on the condition that freedom is given to the colonies and *all* peoples that are dependent, oppressed and deprived of rights. Under the present governments, neither Germany nor Britain and France would accept this condition. In that case, we would have to prepare for and wage a revolutionary war . . . work systematically to bring about an uprising among all . . . colonies and dependent countries in Asia (India, China, Persia etc.), and also, and first and foremost, we would raise up the socialist proletariat of Europe for an insurrection against their governments. There is no doubt that a victory of the Russian proletariat would create extraordinary favourable conditions for the development of the revolution in both Asia and Europe.[24]

Lenin evidently already had in mind what the Bolsheviks of October 1917 saw as the great promise of their revolution.

---

24. 'Several Theses' (*Sotsial-Demokrat*, no. 47 13 October 1915) in Lenin, *Collected Works*, vol. 21 (New York, 1960), p. 403f.

5

The End of the Old Regime

Anyone reviewing events prior to the 'February Revolution' of March 1917 might find the abrupt demise of tsarist Russia surprising, but probably not implausible or incomprehensible. An analysis of the crisis shows that many factors were responsible for the collapse of the autocratic system, the most important of course being the setbacks suffered in the war. (This is not the place to describe them in detail.) The war catalysed the process of internal rot, leaving the ancient state unable to support the extra burdens placed upon it.[1] Already by the summer of 1915, when a German offensive drove the front far eastward, all hope of military victory was apparently lost — unless of course Russia's allies won the war for her.[2]

The human losses were horrendous: eight million dead, wounded, missing or prisoners of war by February 1917. It seemed impossible

---

1. Russia's collapse under the pressure of war has often been described. The best survey in a western language is now T. Hasegawa, *The February Revolution: Petrograd 1917* (Seattle, London, 1981). G. Katkov's study is based on intensive research and a wealth of primary sources: *Russia 1917. The February Revolution* (London, 1967). Though it offers a detailed history of events, many of its assessments are highly suspect and it is marked by earlier controversies originating in the Russian emigration. For specific problems see n.4. A type of Soviet counterpart (emphasising the part played by the masses and the Bolshevik party led by Lenin) was written by the Soviet historian I.I. Mints in his *History of Great October* planned for three volumes: *Istoriya Velikogo Oktyabrya.*, vol. 1, *Sverzhenie samoderzhaviya* (Moscow, 1967).

2. For what follows see the series mentioned in n.1 prepared by Russian *émigré* academics and experts: A.M. Michelson *et al.*, *Russian Public Finance During the War* (1928); S.O. Zagorsky, *State Control of Industry in Russia During the War* (1928); B.E. Nolde, *Russia in the Economic War* (1928); A.N. Antsiferov *et al.*, *Russian Agriculture During the War* (1930); P. Struve *et al.*, *Food Supply in Russia During the War* (1930); N.N. Golovin, *The Russian Army in the War* (1931); S. Kohn *et al.*, *The Costs of the War* (1932). For Russia's financial position see the Soviet interpretation by A.L. Sidorov, *Finansovoe polozhenie Rossii v gody pervoi mirovoi voiny, 1914–1917* (Moscow, 1960). For the 'peasant movement' during the war see the documentation in *Krest'yanskoe dvizhenie v gody pervoi mirovoi voiny. Sbornik dokumentov* (Moscow–Leningrad, 1965). For agricultural production see A.M. Anfinov, *Rossiiskaya derevnya v gody pervoi mirovoi voiny* (Moscow, 1962).

to fill the gaps that had been left. A high percentage of the regular officer corps had been lost in the first year of war and there was no reserve of trained officers to take their place. The army consumed some 350,000 fresh troops each month and they were arriving at the front ever more poorly equipped and often hardly trained. Vast quantities of lost war *matériel* could not be replaced quickly enough. Not until 1916 did Russian industry succeed, with enormous effort, in more or less keeping pace with the mounting needs of an army which was millions strong. There was a shortfall in raw materials and the problems associated with transportation and supply were stupendous. What is more, the state found itself in a hopeless financial position, with the costs of the war estimated at forty million rubles a day in 1916. What is astonishing is that, despite all the setbacks and losses, the Russian military machine continued to function as well as it did until the final collapse of the monarchy.

The hardships behind the front quickly took a turn for the worse, especially in the cities and industrial centres. Food shortages were a grievous problem and rapidly rising prices imposed even greater burdens, especially on the lower classes. War weariness and depression, indifference and despair spread through the population and threatened to burst into rebellions and riots when rumours or provocative slogans reached the masses. The situation was all the more volatile in that the war had altered the composition of the urban proletariat. The old working class had been decimated by the army's hunger for recruits and, as new industrial workers were drawn into the factories, the proportion of women and minors shot upwards. The people thus pressed into industrial service had little sense of purpose or direction, and the waves of strikes which now resumed had an elemental violence and a strange, pre-industrial character very different from the disciplined, well-organised strikes of the prewar period. The countryside too suffered from the war. The burdens it imposed aggravated the woes which these areas had always known. Gradually most able-bodied peasants were drawn out the villages and sent off to the army.

The widening misery could doubtless be described in greater depth and detail. Detailed regional studies could show where and why poverty and dissatisfaction were especially acute. Such an approach would not, however, alleviate concern about whether this method can shed light on the immediate reasons for March 1917. There is nothing specifically Russian about this question, nothing

55

that is peculiar to the Russian Revolution. Elsewhere and in other historical contexts similar difficulties arise when one attempts to offer convincing evidence of the causes of dissatisfaction and instability and the reasons for a high degree of psychological ferment in the general population.[3] These are ongoing problems in historical research. Quantifying methods cannot plumb the factors which contributed to the mass revolutionary insurrection that broke out in the third winter of the war, quickly engulfing the entire country. Statistics on wages, prices and strikes may well show a rising curve and a mounting crisis; however, it would be a mistake to think that the Revolution can be seen 'ripening', as one often reads, and that its development until the final explosion can be traced by carefully accumulating instances of deepening misery. The social psychology of a revolutionary situation can be illustrated of course, but the sum of all the observed phenomena only produces a general impression of the crisis and never an exact measure. The sudden shift in the mass mood from silent suffering and apathy to mass hysteria, wild protest and revolt has an elemental, unconscious quality which cannot be explained rationally. Historians who try to circumscribe and accurately measure the process are poorly advised. That a crisis was brewing could be seen everywhere in the working-class districts of Petrograd, where unrest had been mounting dangerously ever since January 1917. Even here though, a revolt was not being led or even planned. Even Soviet research has now abandoned the absurd thesis that it was the Bolshevik party which induced the masses to converge on the streets. When revolt erupted in the capital and a little later across the country, its vehemence surprised more than those who suddenly found themselves stripped of power. Revolutionaries who had expected and hoped for a sudden sea-change in Russia found their plans overwhelmed by the violence of the storm and themselves tossed about by its waves.[4]

3. See the methodologically important studies by G. Rudé, *The Crowd in the French Revolution* (Oxford, 1959) and *The Crowd in History. A Study of Popular Disturbances in France and England 1730–1848* (New York–London–Sidney, 1964).
4. See the important study by E.N. Burdzhalov, *Vtoraya Russkaya Revolyutsiya. Vosstanie v Petrograde* (The second Russian Revolution. The revolt in Petrograd) (Moscow, 1967). The theory that agents and conspirators played an important role is defended by S. Melgunov among others in *Martovskie dni 1917g.* (Paris, 1961). After the disclosure of the German documents, this point of view gained a firm, new proponent in G. Katkov (cf. n.1). Since Soviet researchers never mention the clearly demonstrable fact that Germany financed Russian revolutionary groups, there is a great temptation in the West to lose all sense of proportion when assessing the true impact of this financing on the events of the Revolution. Katkov's insinuations and

It is much easier to analyse the genesis and evolution of the political conflict that developed during the war between the old regime and the liberal opposition. Much would indicate that the government's decision to go to war was influenced by the traditionally poor relations which existed between state and society. Conservative circles had always maintained that a great war would increase the chances of revolution in Russia and that Petersburg should seek an understanding with Germany in order to forestall this danger and strengthen the monarchy.[5] However, the concern which finally prevailed during the crisis-laden summer of 1914 was that Russia's position as a great power would suffer if she once more failed to take up arms to defend Serbia. What the government feared most of all turned out to be the heavy loss in internal prestige which would result from ceding once again to Austrian demands as well as the ensuing, possibly dangerous increase in support for the political opposition. These concerns were not without foundation. For a long time all shades of liberal opinion had claimed to represent Russia's interests as a great power and had attempted to demonstrate that liberalism was fully compatible with the interests of the state and the nation. The government felt that it could not stand idly by while nationalism was thus appropriated and transformed into a threat to the regime. Autocracy had therefore to continue to be identified with Russian nationalism. In the event, the Tsar's decision to go to war in the middle of the summer of 1914 did seem to stabilise the internal situation. A wave of patriotic emotion swept the country, dispelling old conflicts and even overwhelming some labour leaders.

The consensus created by the war did not last, however. The liberal Kadets in particular (with Paul Milyukov, history professor

---

conclusions amount to a *reductio ad absurdum* of the agent theory. For this question and for the sources see the clear, careful analysis and documentation in W. Hahlweg, *Lenins Rückkehr nach Rußland 1917* (Leiden, 1957); Z.A.B. Zeman, *Germany and the Revolution in Russia* (London, 1958); M. Futrell, *Northern Underground* (London, 1963). See also, for the personality of Parvus-Helphand, W. Scharlau and Z.A.B. Zeman, *Freibeuter der Revolution* (Cologne, 1964). The material presented here should be considered in the light of the accusations against Lenin and the Bolsheviks, first raised in July 1917. G.F. Kennan has shown definitively that the paper published by the US State Department in 1918 on the question of a 'German–Bolshevik conspiracy' was a forgery: 'The Sisson Documents', *Journal of Modern History* XXVII (1956), pp. 130–54.

5. See the memorandum by member of the Council of State P.N. Durnovo (February 1914) in (ed. F.A. Golder), *Documents of Russian History, 1914–1917.* (Gloucester, Mass., repr. 1964), pp. 3–23.

and Duma deputy, as their most eloquent spokeman)[6] expected the government to do more than merely approve of their patriotic loyalty. Liberal gestures and political concessions would have been appropriate, in their view, to acknowledge the bond which had arisen in August 1914 between the Tsar and his people. Organised political forces within society wanted to share with the government more than just the burdens of war; they were persuaded that the nation should be allowed to join in making political decisions. (When they said 'nation' they meant of course themselves.) Many dreams thus seemed closer to realisation and confidence mounted that the war would help revive the movement for political reform that had become bogged down in the pseudo-constitutionalism of 1907. The government had to rely on society for many kinds of support and the public's prospects of extracting this kind of 'accommodation' in return seemed good.

Liberal self-confidence soared for many reasons, not least because tsarist Russia now stood shoulder to shoulder with England and republican France. For years liberals had been adjuring the government not to revert to a conservative monarchs' league; now that danger had apparently passed. Liberal affinity for English parliamentarism seemed to find official sanction with Russia securely within the Entente. Furthermore, a wartime alliance with the parliamentary democracies was likely to further the political modernisation process in Russia and help dismantle autocracy and the omnipotent bureaucracy. Liberal political sentiments were also affected by a desire to draw a clear distinction between the system in Russia and the monarchical systems in Germany and Austria. When conversation turned to the struggle against the 'Germanic despotism' of the Hohenzollerns, liberals craved no longer to feel ashamed that Russia too was ruled by a despot. Changes were clearly necessary if Russian society was to come to a modern, ideological understanding of the significance of the war. Liberals therefore cherished an internal war aim as well: constitutional, parliamentary monarchy, the programme which had been frustrated in peacetime.[7]

Developments during the war cannot have pleased those who nurtured such hopes. The government did all it could to keep the nation's representatives in the Duma on a short leash and to dissi-

---

6. For Milyukov's interpretation of the Revolution see *Istoriya Vtoroi Russkoi Revolyutsii* (Sofia, 1921–3) as well as his posthumously published memoirs; *Vospominaniia 1859–1917* (New York, 1955), vol. 2.
7. Cf. Chapter 3.

pate any political momentum it developed. The enthusiasm of the 'people's representatives' was expected to exhaust itself on routine bills of little consequence. The Duma was to remain an isolated, impotent appendix of the autocratic bureaucracy and not be allowed to develop new powers in novel directions. Conflicts were most apparent when the bureaucracy clashed with the self-governing institutions — bodies which had been strengthened as the zemstvos and municipalities had taken over a number of tasks clearly vital to the war effort. These included much of the provisioning of the army, relief for populations which had fled or been evacuated and for invalids and war dependents, public charity, collections and donations for the war and, last but not least, many medical and hospital services. In May 1915 a third institution was added to the zemstvos and municipalities, the result of an initiative taken by leading industrialists. The so-called war industry committees were intended to reduce the catastrophic shortage of war *matériel* by means of more effective organisation of production and transportation. In addition, efforts were made to consult worker representatives in order to instil discipline and good work habits in Russian factories and to resolve social conflicts by seeking a consensus through public institutions. It was highly significant that the institutions of organised society spread during the summer of 1915 beyond the provincial and local levels to the central, all-Russian level. An all-Russian Zemstvo Union, All-Russian Town Union and Central War Industries Committee appeared. Attempts were made to coordinate regional activities in joint bureaus, committees and conferences and close relations were established between the three central organs of self-government.[8]

The central government was forced to accept these new institutions because the bureaucracy could not provide the services which they offered. However, permission was granted only reluctantly, on condition that these institutions not extend their activities too far. The relationship between the government and these bodies remained disingenuous and unpleasant, shot through with distrust, jealousy and mutual disdain. The problems they experienced in working together could be seen every day in the mixed commissions which the government established to 'discuss and co-ordinate

8. T.J. Polner, *Russian Local Government During the War and the Union of Zemstvos* (New Haven, 1930); P.P. Gronsky, N.J. Astrov, *The War and the Russian Government* (New Haven, 1928). For the Soviet view of the role of the 'bourgeoisie' see P. Volobuev, *Proletariat i burzhuaziya Rossii 1917g.* (Moscow, 1964).

measures for the defence of the state'. Representatives of the self-governing bodies remained convinced that the central bureaucracy was detracting substantially from the energy the public might have thrown into the war effort.

Some of the disputes which erupted over the technical means needed to continue the work of these public institutions manifested clear political overtones. There was close co-operation and many personal ties of course between the institutions and the parties in the Duma, although party politics were not practised in the self-governing bodies. Nevertheless, speakers in the Duma now had a much stronger sense than before 1914 that they enjoyed the backing of a public movement (institutionalised in the zemstvos, municipalities and industrial committees) which lent them added weight in their dealings with the government.

When the military débâcle of the summer of 1915 became obvious, the hostility between the government and the majority in the Duma — between the Autocracy and public opinion — rose to a dangerous pitch. It was widely assumed that the government was totally incapable of bringing the war to a victorious conclusion. The authority of the Tsar and the government was in a state of continuous decline and grumblings which could not be voiced openly were inflated by rumour into apocalyptic visions. Besides military failure, the apparent end of all governmental activity bears most of the responsibility for the wave of protest:[9] the regime appeared frivolous and irresponsible. It apparently had no interest in rallying the nation to create a mighty, unified force and in working towards victory in partnership with the people (by which was usually understood the Duma).

There were indeed many indications of an almost pathological collapse during the war years: unparalleled abuses in an administration crippled by bitter rivalry with the military command; an unbridled, overweening police apparatus; repeated humiliation of the well-intentioned movements which arose in society; scandal

9. For the crisis during the summer of 1915 see primarily the notes of cabinet secretary A.N. Yakhontov on the meetings of the Council of Ministers: *Arkhiv Russkoi Revolyutsii XVIII* (Berlin, 1926), pp. 15–136 — now available in English translation in (ed. M. Cherniavsky), *Prologue to Revolution*. (Englewood Cliffs, N.J., 1967). For the liberal opposition see T. Riha, 'Miliukov and the Progressive Bloc in 1915', *Journal of Modern History* XXXII (1960), pp. 16ff., as well as the archival publications of B.B. Grave, *Burzhuaziya nakanune fevral'skoi revolyutsii* (The bourgeoisie on the eve of the February Revolution) (Moscow–Leningrad, 1927). Excerpts in Golder, *Documents of Russian History, 1914–1917.*

surrounding Minister of War Sukhomlinov; the hair-raising in-
trigues of the court camarilla with the 'German Tsarina' from
Darmstadt; Rasputin, the brutal, debauched monk, miracle worker
and *éminence grise* of the regime; 'dark forces' believed to be
agitating for a separate peace with Germany[10] and ultimately the
weak, hollow-cheeked Tsar who allowed himself to be pushed time
and again by the divinely inspired admonitions of his consort into
foolish demonstrations of his omnipotence. In August 1915 he was
even persuaded to take personal command over the army and to
send Nikolashka (Nikolai Nikolaevich), his uncle and the supreme
commander of the Russian forces who had displeased the Tsarina,
to the Caucasus.[11] Nicholas cut a curious figure as a monarch. His
limited but by no means malevolent mind always seemed to mal-
function when the time came to seek a compromise with the Duma
and grant concessions to society. Taken together, all these factors
precipitated a profound crisis of confidence, mounting resistance
from the oppostion and the increasing isolation of the Tsar from the
people around him and from the levers of power.

The nation's plight was clearly evident in the crisis-ridden summer of 1915 when a group of deputies succeeded in organising a
broad opposition front in the Duma and in rallying a cohesive
majority behind an explicit political programme. This new attempt
at a unified oppostion deemed itself the 'Progressive Bloc'. The
Kadets were joined by those Octobrists who had outlived pseudo-
constitutionalism, deputies from entrepreneurial circles, the so-
called 'Progressives' and a number of staunch conservatives who
dubbed themselves 'Progressive Nationalists'. Some members of the
Council of State, that worthy chamber of notables, joined the ranks.
Only the extreme Right and the small socialist parties — barely
one-quarter of all deputies — failed to adhere to the alliance.[12]
Although the Duma had been created as a rubber stamp institution,
a majority now stood in open opposition to the regime. The

10. Soviet historians have now dropped the claim that the Russians made a serious
attempt to arrange a separate peace, cf. Burdzhalov, *Vtoraya Russkaya Revolyutsiya*,
p. 72. For German policies see F. Fischer, *Germany's War Aims in the First World
War* (London, 1969); E. Zechlin, 'Friedensbestrebungen und Revolutionierungsver-
suche', *Aus Politik und Zeitgeschehen*. Supplement to *Das Parlament* B20 (1961), B
24–5 (1961), B 20 and 22 (1963).
11. Cf. the correspondance of the royal couple, *The Letters of the Tsar to the
Tsaritsa 1914–1917* (London, 1929); *Pis'ma imperatritsy Aleksandry Feodorovny k
imp. Nikolayu II* (Berlin, 1922); J. Kühn (ed.), *Die Letzte Zarin* (Berlin, 1922).
12. See the documentation in F.A. Golder (ed.), *Documents of Russian History,
1914–17*, pp. 78ff.

opposition programme was very moderate and only seemed provocative because of the Autocracy's insistence that even the most modest reform, the most insignificant concession, was too dangerous or unacceptable in principle. According to the reformers, only a 'strong, firm and active authority' could 'lead the motherland to victory', an authority 'based on the confidence of the people and able to secure the co-operation of all citizens'.[13]

The tone grew less decisive when the time came to set out concrete proposals about the means to achieve these ends. The opposition demanded that 'a government be formed by people who enjoy the confidence of the country' and who would be willing to work in partnership with the legislative chambers. There were no demands, therefore, for a parliamentary government drawn from the ranks of the Duma, and no one was so impolitic as to point out that they had been elected according to the restrictive curial franchise of 1907. Nevertheless, the entire catalogue of proposals evinced a strong drift in the direction of liberalism and constitutionalism: an executive fully subject to the fundamental laws, guaranteed political and civic freedoms, a generous amnesty, a solution to the Polish question that would increase national autonomy, restoration of Finnish autonomy, repeal of legal disabilities affecting non-Russian nationalities, especially Jews and 'Little Russians', legal equality for peasants, legalisation of union activities and the labour press and finally revision of the self-government statute and the municipal code in order to extend the competence of the zemstvos and municipalities and to rescind the reactionary electoral laws of 1890–2. The deputies in the self-governing institutions would thus become more representative of the entire population.[14]

A list of ministers considered suitable for a war cabinet was already circulating in the corridors of the Duma. Stiff, senile Prime Minister Goremykin would be replaced by the President of the Duma, Rodzianko and a number of important ministries would be taken over by prominent representatives of the Progressive Bloc — distinguished members of the opposition, many of whom were to take their place in the Provisional Government of March 1917: Milyukov, Guchkov, Konovalov, Shingarev and Nekrasov. Consultations were already underway with individual ministers in the generally despised government who were considered progressive or

13. From the programme of the 'Progressive Bloc', cited in Hellmann, p. 79.
14. Ibid.

willing to assist in restructuring the cabinet. However, deaf old Goremykin refused to resign out of loyalty to the Tsar, despite pressure from within his own cabinet. Only in January 1916 did he finally go, with the gracious permission of the Tsar, in favour of Boris Stürmer, a man with a German name who was chosen not by the Progressive Bloc but by Rasputin and the Tsarina as their puppet. Even well-disposed observers were horrified at the decisions of the emotionally unstable court camarilla, with its baffling reliance on divine inspiration in the naming of ministers. When Foreign Minister Sazonov was dismissed in July 1916, as a result of tensions over the Allies' demand for Polish autonomy, the state was left bereft of advisors with a reasonably good understanding of political affairs. The long-suffering ambassadors of England and France experienced great difficulty thereafter in swallowing their own doubts and persuading their governments of Russia's good will and continuing loyalty to the alliance.[15]

Despite a crisis of confidence which seemed to grow worse from month to month, the opposition did not alter its political programme of the summer of 1915 before the Revolution. What intensified was not the substance of opposition demands but the emotion behind them. Spokesmen for the Zemstvo Union, the Town Union and the industrial committees had long previously thrown their support behind the majority motion in the Duma in a round of eloquent declarations and stirring appeals. The despair of frustrated opposition members reached unparalleled proportions in the autumn of 1916. Russian war aims, which these men appeared to support, had slipped beyond reach with the failure of the Brusilov offensive. Enemy forces had penetrated deep into the motherland. Berlin and Vienna, not Petrograd, were preparing to confer a (rather suspect) independence on the Polish people. Defeat in Serbia and on the Romanian front meant that the Slavonic Balkan territories, which Russia felt should be subject to its control were well beyond grasp. Repeated assurances that the Allies were certain to fulfil their treaty obligations provided the only remaining hope that the Patriarchal cross of the one true faith would soon adorn St Sophia and the Russian eagle would command the Straits. No real expectation existed that these prizes would one day fall to the superiority of Russian arms. In a bitter attack, the opposition formulated the

---

15. Notes and memoirs of diplomats: M. Paléologue, *Am Zarenhof während des Weltkrieges* (Munich, 1925); G. Buchanan, *Meine Mission in Rußland* (Berlin, 1926).

Russian version of the stab-in-the-back myth. 'Is this folly or treason?' Milyukov, leader of Kadets, demanded to know in November 1916 in a famous question from the tribune of the Duma. There was no need for an answer. Everyone who heard Milyukov's words knew what the public had long believed: it was treason, a conspiracy of dark forces at the Court and in the private apartments of the Empress. 'German poison' was at work, a German party determined to ruin Russia.[16] As unrealistic as such suspicions were, the truth was grim enough. In October 1916 strikes, especially in Petrograd, for the first time became as intense as they had been on the eve of the war. The political agitation which the committees of the Social Democratic party were still capable of sustaining created a feeling that the winter would be difficult. The shadows of 1905 reared their heads,[17] and many in the Progressive Bloc were haunted by the fear that the people would again take to the streets.

Might the catastrophe have been avoided? The agony of the regime might appear to have been little more than a tragedy confined to the royal family — a morbid, hysterical Tsarina convinced of Rasputin's powers of prophecy and a helpless, fatalistic Tsar who watched without apparent concern or resistance as his authority slipped away. Such an interpretation gains credence from a movement which arose in opposition circles in the late autumn of 1916 and which aimed to compel the Tsar, by persuasion or if necessary by force, to abdicate in favour of his son. In the end, though the plan was a bold one, the will to act was wanting.[18] The general sense of crisis also affected many Russian generals who felt that a catastrophe was near — though not because any military disaster seemed likely in the near future. Army commanders believed that the army was capable of defending itself satisfactorily and even of mounting a fresh offensive in the spring of 1917.[19] At a joint military conference held in Petrograd in January and February, Russia's allies were assured that such plans were in preparation. What senior military officers feared above all was the lack of strong political leadership, the feeling that the government was disintegrating without anything

16. See the expurgated version of the speech in Golder, *Documents of Russian History, 1914–1917*, pp. 154ff. Also, P.N. Milyukov, *Vospominaniia*, Part II, pp. 277ff. Details in G. Katkov, *Russia 1917. The February Revolution*, pp. 187ff.
17. Cf. Burdzhalov's interpretation (n.4), pp. 56ff., 81ff.
18. Burdzhalov, pp. 77ff., Katkov, pp. 173ff.
19. For the state of the army on the eve of the Revolution see more recently, A.K. Wildman, *The End of the Russian Imperial Party* (Princeton, NJ, 1980), pp. 75ff.; G. Wettig, 'Die Rolle der Armee im revolutionären Machtkampf 1917', *Forschungen zur osteuropäischen Geschichte* 12 (1967), pp. 65ff.

to replace it. Even the Grand Dukes begged the Tsar to pull himself together for the sake of the nation, to take decisive action to restore the crippled authority of the government and to begin governing personally again in order to do everything possible to repair his severely damaged relationship with the public. As is well known, a young relative of the Tsar was involved in the monarchist conspiracy to assassinate Rasputin in December 1916.[20]

The paralysis of the old regime was the only outcome. A small band of Duma politicians, more desperate than violent, continued to weave plans for a palace coup. Yet they always hesitated to act. Nicholas, operating in complete isolation, broke off his last contacts with political forces within the Empire and spent his final few days as Tsar poring over routine business at imperial headquarters. At the end of February, a mass revolutionary insurrection of the working class and the Petrograd garrison erupted with elemental fury. Just a few days later, the countryside and the armies at the front were engulfed. The Tsar proved incapable of mounting a response and spent his time countersigning senseless orders in an effort to mask his bewilderment. No one but his sick wife was at his side to counsel him not to capitulate. All those who had previously spoken to him in the name of the people now saw abdication as the only hope of forestalling violent revolution and a collapse into anarchy. This would clear the way for parliamentary government by the centrist parties in the Duma, for a government enjoying the confidence of the people.[21] However, without waiting to be invited, the people now began to converge on the streets determined to speak for themselves. Many politicians had already guessed what the chilling message would be: the public had no confidence in His Majesty's worthy opposition and no mandate to confer on it.

The question has often been asked as to whether the abrupt collapse of the Autocracy could have been avoided if the Russian Empire had had at its helm a stronger monarch than Nicholas II. Such 'what if' questions can be raised but never satisfactorily answered. One can certainly imagine that the final demise of tsarist Russia would not have occurred in this manner if the monarch had sought an early settlement with the Duma and those sectors of

20. For a detailed portrait of Rasputin see Katkov, pp. 196–210; for the inter-Allied conference, R.D. Warth, *The Allies and the Russian Revolution. From the Fall of the Monarchy to the Peace of Brest–Litovsk* (Durham, N.C., 1954), pp. 18ff.
21. Cf. the autobiography of the President of the Duma M.V. Rodzianko, *Erinnerungen* (Berlin, n.d.) as well as *Arkhiv Russkoi Revolyutsii* VI, pp. 5–80. For the attitude of army commanders, see *Arkhiv Russkoi Revolyutsii* III, pp. 247–70.

society represented in the self-governing bodies. However, other considerations outweigh this view, which reduces the history of the Revolution to a question of personalities. If one examines the historical situation, it seems unlikely that the old regime would have been able in any case to assume the task of political reconstruction and adaptation under the pressure of war. For years the Autocracy had identified itself with permanence, not change. The Tsar's behaviour seems therefore to reflect more the general conviction of the old regime than a historical accident or quirk of fate. The old order was inflexible and the only opportunity for survival it could perceive was to cling to its traditional foundations. Every step off the beaten track was considered to be fraught with dangers which could no longer be controlled. The debilitating compulsion to resist innovation turned out to have fateful consequences when the war mobilised the political will of the public. The regime proved incapable of rallying, unable to rally even those social strata which considered themselves to be the 'pillars of the nation'.

Another consideration should be mentioned in this context, namely the possibilities and limitations inherent in the renewal which the opposition sought with such vigour and eloquence. The much vaunted reconciliation of the Tsar with his people probably could not have survived the social realities of Russia, at least not in the manner in which the politicians in the Duma understood it. The Russian people did not and could not possibly have taken part in the dispute raging between the Autocracy and the opposition, even though each side liked to identify itself with the people. A means had therefore to be found to include the massed ranks of the lower classes in the new political arrangement; the Tsar in other words had to be reconciled with much more of the nation than just liberals, progressives and their supporters. For many years the Autocracy had acted as an effective integrating force on the whole of Russian society. Reformers wishing to alter the political system would have had to find a way to fulfil this function. However, the reformers neither knew nor concerned themselves with popular feelings and expectations. A nation craving peace was instructed by its political leaders that Constantinople still had to be captured. After that victory even more unredeemed war aims remained. Hence the Russian opposition was no closer to the people than the tsarist bureaucracy or senior military officials. The opposition was rooted in an upper class for which the broad mass of the population felt no attachment and with which it had no relationship as natural as its relationship with the Tsar had once been. The most passionate speeches of well-meaning lawyers and professors could not have bridged the gulf between those at the top and those at the bottom — a gulf running through Russian history and one which even the official Orthodox religion[22] was unable to span. In any case, no one was prepared even to speak to the masses below. The rift between ruler and educated classes should not therefore blind one to the even wider rift which existed between two entirely separate social worlds. When viewed from below, the clever gentlemen who fenced with the Tsar resembled him much more than they would ever have imagined. It would never have occurred to the peasants, workers and common soldiers that they could have formed a mutually supportive community, a 'society' with the social worlds above. The year 1917 made this perfectly clear.

22. J.S. Curtiss, *Church and State in Russia. The Last Years of the Empire 1900–1917* (New York, 1940).

6

Democracy in Crisis

With Nicholas clearly at the end of the road, Duma deputies Guchkov and Shulgin journeyed to meet the royal carriage at Pskov and returned to Petrograd with the Tsar's official abdication.[1] In this historic document, Nicholas renounced on behalf of himself and his young son Aleksei 'the crown of the Russian Empire and supreme authority ... with the approval of the imperial Duma'. The line of succession was transferred to Nicholas's brother, the Grand Duke Mikhail Aleksandrovich. The latter, who resided in the capital and knew full well which way the wind was blowing, immediately declined. He officially informed the Duma deputation which met with him in a house on the Millionaya that he would accept the throne only if such was the 'will of all our people' as determined by a constituent assembly elected by universal, secret, direct and equal suffrage. It would be the task of this assembly to determine the will of the people and to decide on the future form of government.[2] The Russian people to whom the Grand Duke deferred never again expressed a desire to return to monarchism.

On 3 (16) March 1917 not only 'tsarism' ceased to exist but monarchy also. Many deputies had been pleading in the previous weeks and months for 'a government enjoying the confidence of the people', but none of them had ever envisaged such a result, certainly not the gentlemen of the Progressive Bloc. What they had sought was parliamentary government under the monarchy and a cabinet composed of centrist deputies from the Duma who could have

---

1. See the notes of V.V. Shul'gin (Schulgin): *Tage* (Berlin, 1928). For Shul'gin himself, see the excerpts from his pre-1917 memoirs in *Istoriya SSSR* (1966), no. 6, pp. 70–91 and (1967) no. 1, pp. 123–44.
2. For Nicholas's official abdication and Grand Duke Michael's renunciation of the throne see the documentation in *The Provisional Government 1917. Documents.* Selected and edited by R.P. Browder and A.F. Kerensky (Stanford, 1961), vol. 1, pp. 83ff. See also details in G. Katkov, *Russia 1917. The February Revolution*, pp. 306–58.

successfully pursued the war against the Central Powers. To eradicate the monarchy struck them as extremely unwise — if only because an authoritative figure raised above party seemed to exert a palliative effect on the simple people and to distract them from the absence of real democracy. Now however, constitutional expectations such as these were quashed forever in the course of a few days in February during which crowds numbering several hundred thousand converged on the streets of the capital and joined forces with the regiments of the Petrograd Military District. The insurrection of workers and soldiers overwhelmed the deputies in the Duma[3] and no one could say where it would eventually deposit liberals and abandoned monarchists.

Some of the power which slipped so unexpectedly from the hands of the old regime fell to the majority coalition in the Duma. Suddenly this hobbled embodiment of Russian parliamentarism was free. Its most prominent representatives pressed to gain new authority and it seemed that they might succeed. Under pressure from the insurrectionary situation, the Council of Elders had already taken an important step in this direction on 27 February (12 March) when it resisted the Tsar's order to prorogue the Duma and instead instituted a 'Provisional Committee of the Duma' in the Tauride Palace. This body was composed of deputies from the ranks of the Progressive Bloc as well as two socialists, A.F. Kerensky from the Socialist Revolutionary faction of the Trudoviki (Labour group) and the Georgian Chkheidze, a Menshevik Social Democrat. Duma President Rodzianko presided over the Committee. It promised to restore order and called on the population to 'assist in the difficult task of creating a new government'. The Committee tacitly assumed that the cabinet appointed by the Tsar under the bland Prince Golitsyn had been disbanded, in fact as well as in appearance. This assumption amounted to a *coup d'état*, forced upon the Committee by the situation in the capital. The Duma either had to enter the power vacuum or be swept away by the violence of the revolution. Rodzianko had implored the Tsar by telegram to accord the Provisional Committee his official approval since it could not be legit-

3. For the evolution of the uprising see G. Wettig, 'Die Rolle der Armee', pp. 84ff.; M. Ferro (who includes a large amount of Soviet research), *La révolution de 1917. La chute du tsarisme et les origines d'octobre* (Paris, 1967), pp. 63ff. For the portrayal of the uprising as resulting from German machinations see Katkov, *Russia 1917. The February Revolution*, pp. 247ff.; for the Soviet interpretation see I.I. Mints, *Istoriya Velikogo Oktyabrya* (Moscow, 1967), vol. 1, pp. 437ff., and E.N. Burdzhalov, *Vtoraya Russkaya Revolyutsiya* (Moscow, 1967), pp. 94ff.

imised otherwise, either on the basis of the Fundamental Laws or the Duma's own rules of procedure. However, the Tsar failed to respond. If the Committee was to act, it would have to rely on the acclamation of the masses — the workers and soldiers now parading *en masse* through the Tauride Palace in order to persuade themselves of their victory over the old regime.[4]

The initiative undertaken by the Duma was not without a competing claim. In a momentous step, a handful of socialist deputies and labour leaders had succeeded in establishing contact with the new revolutionary public and to some extent in guiding the mass upheaval. These men had also been prompted to take action by conditions in the capital. The factional disputes which had previously divided them now seemed insignificant in the face of the Revolution. Only a few hours before the Provisional Committee of the Duma was proclaimed, a meeting in the Tauride Palace decided spontaneously that a soviet of deputies similar to the workers' soviet of 1905 should be constituted in order to represent the workers and mutinous soldiers of Petrograd.[5] Thus a major revolutionary institution emerged on the flank of the Provisional Committee. This soviet resolved to do what the Committee could not because of its composition: that is, represent the revolutionary people and express its will. As it stated in its first appeal, the soviet

> has taken on the task of organising the strength of the people and of struggling for political freedom and government by the people. . . . Together and in alliance with our troops we wish to destroy completely the old regime and convoke a constituent assembly chosen by equal, direct, general and secret elections.[6]

Every factory and company of soldiers in Petrograd was to elect one deputy to the soviet and larger factories sent one deputy for every

4. There is extensive documentation of the events: Browder and Kerensky (eds.), *The Provisional Government 1917. Documents*, vol. I, pp. 39ff.; Golder, *Documents of Russian History*, pp. 280ff. For an informative survey of the entire Revolution see the account, first published in 1935, of the American journalist H.W. Chamberlin: *The Russian Revolution, 1917–1921*, (2 vols., New York, 1947).

5. For this and what follows see O. Anweiler, *Die Rätebewegung in Rußland, 1905–1921* (Leiden, 1958), pp. 127ff. *Russia 1917.*, M. Ferro, *La révolution de 1917*, pp. 77ff., Katkov, pp. 359ff., Burdzhalov, *Vtoraya Russkaya Revolyutsiya*, pp. 242ff. See in addition the famous memoirs of the socialist writer N.N. Sukhanov who was close to M. Gorky: *Zapiski o revolyutsii* (parts 1–7, Berlin, 1922/23). For a shorter German version see N. Ehlert (ed.), *Tagebuch der russischen Revolution* (Munich, 1967).

6. Cited in Hellmann, dtv 227/8, p. 128.

1,000 workers. These stipulations immediately lent a predominantly military cast to the Petrograd Soviet of Workers' and Soldiers' Deputies. It was hoped that this would win over the common soldier. When the vast assembly finally convened in the second half of March some 2,000 soldiers' deputies attended but only approximately 800 workers' deputies. The military element continued to dominate both the ensuing 'All-Russian Conference' of soviet deputies and the All-Russian Congress of Soviets held in June.

A prime concern of the Petrograd Soviet had already emerged by 1 March (i.e. before the abdication of the Tsar) when it issued its famous *Prikaz* (Order) No. 1:[7] the support of the troops had to be secured. Some fears still existed that the 'dark forces' of reaction could succeed in reversing the rapid victory which had been gained, so steps needed to be taken to ensure the success of the Revolution in the countryside and at the front after the initial breakthrough in Petrograd. Orders from the Soviet proved to be an effective instrument in this campaign by sanctioning efforts to democratise the army through revolt. Though there was talk about preserving strict military discipline in the armed forces, the guidelines issued by the Soviet confirmed the officer corps' loss of authority and the end of all traditional military discipline. Henceforth all military orders had to pass revolutionary scrutiny by the elected soldiers' committees which surfaced in all sections of the army and by the Soviet of Workers' and Soldiers' Deputies. The Soviet called upon all units to submit to it and to refuse to obey all commands that conflicted with its decisions and orders. The Provisional Committee of the Duma proved to countermand this signal to dissolve the old army. With Order No. 1, the Soviet of Workers' and Soldiers' Deputies gained *de facto* power — not only in Petrograd but far into the countryside.

Events in the capital were soon duplicated throughout Russia.[8] Soviets everywhere proved their usefulness as a unifying and organising force whenever the people began to involve themselves in events. However, the soviets did not destroy or replace the institutions which had taken root under the old regime. Instead the two systems co-existed cheek by jowl. The most striking example of this

---

7. For the text, *ibid.*, p. 133. For the development of Order No. 1 see G. Wettig, 'Die Rolle der Armee', pp. 148ff.; A.K. Wildman, *The End of the Russian Imperial Army* (Princeton, 1980), pp. 121ff.
8. O. Anweiler, *Die Rätebewegung in Rußland*, pp. 136ff., I.I. Mints, *Istoriya Velikogo Oktyabrya*, vol. 1, pp. 755ff.

was in Petrograd, at the epicentre of the Revolution. Here, despite the preponderance of power which had fallen to the Soviet from the outset, a strange confrontation evolved and became the hallmark of emergency democracy after the collapse of the monarchy. In one corner was the Provisional Committee of the Duma, a wellspring of liberalism and remnant of tsarist times which had turned revolutionary in response to pressure from below; in the other corner stood the Soviet of Workers' and Soldiers' Deputies, the symbol of the Revolution and the major forum of 'revolutionary democracy' as defined by the deputies from the socialist parties. This dual, highly inequitable arrangement of soviets and more traditional organs of self-government developed not just in Petrograd but also at the local level, in the provinces and districts where small landholders began to congregate in peasant soviets and soon joined forces with soldiers' and workers' soviets.[9] This parallel system — bourgeois, democratic institutions on the one hand and soviets embodying lower-class interests on the other — reveals a democratic order which was still improvised and incomplete. Once again the traditional gulf was apparent between the organised political forces of the old society and the broad masses which were just now entering the political arena in the wake of the Revolution.[10]

The most significant outgrowth of this constellation of forces was the Provisional Government, created on 3 (16) March after tortuous negotiations between the Provisional Committee and representatives of the Soviet.[11] Remarkably, the cabinet was composed not of a coalition but of a liberal group from the centre of the Progressive Bloc. It was presided over by Prince G.E. Lvov, chairman of the Zemstvo Union. Milyukov, leader of the Kadets, was appointed Foreign Minister and Guchkov, an Octobrist who had long maintained good connections with Russian generals, became Minister of War. The interests of capital were represented by the textile magnate, Konovalov, who became Minister of Trade and Industry and by the sugar millionaire, Tereshchenko (Minister of Finance). The only member of the cabinet to have ties both with the Provisional Government and the Soviet was A.F. Kerensky who was appointed

---

9. Anweiler, *Die Rätebewegung*, pp. 147ff., Mints, pp. 858ff.
10. The feelings and expectations of various sections of the population are investigated, using newly discovered archival material, by M. Ferro, *La révolution de 1917*, pp. 170ff. (Les 'Cahiers de la révolution russe'); for views within the army see again Wettig, 'Die Rolle der Armee', pp. 186ff.
11. Cf. Browder and Kerensky, vol. I., pp. 117ff., Ferro, pp. 243ff., Katkov, pp. 375ff., Burdzhalov, pp. 308ff., Sukhanov, *Tagebuch*, pp. 167ff.

Minister of Justice. This thirty-six year old lawyer had developed his considerable rhetorical skills while occupying a place on the extreme left of the Duma. At a time when history had become theatre and the pathos of skilled agitators was deciding questions of state, Kerensky was indispensible both to the government and to the Soviet. Although he entered the government as a vice-president of the Soviet, the latter did not wish openly to declare that it was participating in a coalition. Lvov's cabinet nevertheless had the appearance of an alliance because it depended on the political credibility which only the Soviet could lend the liberal government — a situation similar to that in France during the 1930s when popular front governments were supported by the French Communist Party even though it was not represented within the cabinet. The leadership of the Soviet thus participated in an arm's length coalition which could be revoked like any formal alliance. The Soviet hoped that its reticence would be interpreted as a sign of its continuing distrust of a bourgeois partner and as an expression of revolutionary vigilance.

The first public declaration of the new government revealed the initial results of this understanding between 'bourgeois democracy' and 'revolutionary democracy'. Important traces of the liberal programme were still evident, but they were largely obscured by the radically democratic demands which the Petrograd Soviet had imposed on the liberal ministers in the packed committee rooms of the Tauride Palace: a complete and immediate amnesty covering all political and religious offences, including terrorist attacks, military revolts etc.; the widest imaginable political freedoms; the abolition of all legal disparities between classes, religious groups and nationalities; immediate preparations for the rapid convocation of a freely elected constituent assembly; complete democratisation of the organs of local self-government and the creation of a people's militia to replace the police; the freeing of soldiers from all legal restrictions and, finally, guarantees that the military units which had taken part in the revolution would not be disarmed or removed from the capital.[12]

This programme had been thrust on the liberals under crisis conditions and it left many questions unanswered. What was clear was that the Provisional Government could not govern or issue any decrees without the consent of the Soviet and that the government

12. Text in Hellmann, pp. 152ff.

was being forced to carry out a revolution that was not of its design or making. Those liberals who became ministers were the creations of the Revolution rather than active participants in it. They were at the mercy of elemental forces which could not be subdued by cabinet resolutions, though they might be perhaps by the Soviet. As a result, the Provisional Government suffered from chronic weaknesses. However, its attempts to hold firm and to gain sufficient power to act independently were not without hope. The socialist politicians in the Petrograd Soviet also had to bow before the constraints of the times. So long as the new freedoms were not safe from the threat of a return to autocratic government and so long as Russia was at war, both the Provisional Government and the Soviet still had a common interest in warding off their internal and external enemies.

The question has often been raised as to why the Soviet went along with this intrigue and did not take steps to replace the liberal government. The socialists' reticence can be explained only in part by their often stated ideological conviction that this was a 'bourgeois revolution' and that the bourgeoisie had therefore to take the lead. The soviet leaders were apparently not yet fully cognisant of their power and the political uses to which it could be put. They had suddenly been liberated from gaol and the underground, from banishment and isolation and had been swept into power. Consequently, they had not yet found time to establish an identity and to align themselves. Furthermore, socialists felt isolated and alienated from the very state which was now theirs for the taking. Although the heart of the old state had been plucked out and its omnipotence and oppressiveness were but memories, the institutional machinery remained intact. Most of the civil service had not been replaced and the successor government had inherited a host of old tasks and obligations. The soviet deputies wished for no contact with the former regime and were extremely reluctant to seize control of an apparatus which was still largely intact. In addition, the skill required to operate the complex machinery of state could not be acquired overnight.

The soviets did not therefore try to penetrate the state bureaucracy. Instead they were satisfied with tight, outside control. They could reduce it to paralysis, but they had no intention of overthrowing it. The Petrograd Soviet remained convinced that government and the responsibilities of state were not its concern but that of the liberals. For the rest, the Soviet assured itself and others that the anaemic government would be subject to revolutionary discipline and would be compelled to provide the kind of 'revolutionary democracy' which the masses demanded. While the revolutionaries waited for the Constituent Assembly to be convened, their determination to remould Russia was held in abeyance. They felt bound by the norms of a parliamentary democracy which did not yet exist. The result of this *attentisme* was a curious mutual dependence between the government and the Soviet. The term 'dual power', coined to describe this situation, is rather misleading. Those who were supposed to rule did not have the support of the masses and never really held power while those on whom the Revolution had conferred power did not want to exercise it.

An ambiguous relationship towards power was therefore the hallmark of the political parties which enjoyed an absolute majority in the Petrograd Soviet and a little later in the countryside. The consequences would be momentous. This same sort of problem also surfaced within the parties committed to 'revolutionary democracy'. The Socialist Revolutionaries found many new adherents among the 'peasants in uniform' as well as among broad sections of the rural population, but this new, mass support simply overwhelmed them.[13] When suddenly confronted with unexpectedly large numbers of sympathisers, the Socialist Revolutionaries turned out to have goals and plans which were impractical, though the object of much passionate debate. Far from helping to clarify the party's strategy, the Revolution revealed its confusion; instead of steering events, the SRs were dragged along in their wake. Even within the leadership wide differences of opinion emerged as to the direction which their radicalism should take. In order to compensate for this drift and the lack of clear political goals, party members developed empty slogans to provide at least a temporary focus for their heterogeneous movement. Those inclined to listen were promised the dawn of a new age of democracy for working people. The traditional promise to effect radical change in agriculture was reduced to the slogan 'land and freedom'. 'Nationalisation' and 'socialisation' amounted to much the same thing and expressions of Russian patriotism were added to the mix. The resulting babble of catch-phrases quickly drowned out any attempt on the part of a few

13. The standard work is O.H. Radkey, *The Agrarian Foes of Bolshevism. Promise and Default of the Russian Socialist Revolutionaries 1917* (New York, 1958); see the account of the party's leading light: V. Chernov, *The Great Russian Revolution* (New York, 1936).

isolated individuals to arrive at clear political decisions.

Like all party leaders, the SRs attempted to postpone the hopes and expectations of the Russian people until the projected Constituent Assembly could meet. Only then would the dreams of the people be realised. The astonishingly broad support enjoyed by the Socialist Revolutionaries was due not to their persuasive presentation of socialist theory but to their skill at capturing in slogans and catchwords the elemental, irrational mood of the people. While the SRs thus gave voice to the emotion and pathos of the revolution, they failed to develop an effective revolutionary strategy. The result was a party that was strong but highly vulnerable. Its support could easily dissipate when the inevitable collision with political reality finally arrived.

The second important party in the Petrograd Soviet was the Social Democratic Party, represented primarily by its Menshevik wing, both in the soviets and the labour unions. The Mensheviks were intellectuals and labour leaders who interpreted the collapse of tsarism as a preliminary historical goal which had long been desired:[14] the 'bourgeois revolution' had finally arrived. It brought with it 'a complete victory for democracy' and a promise of freedom not only for the proletariat but for 'all living movements in the country'. The Russian people had now attained what it had failed to achieve in 1905. According to the laws of history as interpreted by the Mensheviks, the bourgeoisie would necessarily have to take over the reins of government at this stage in Russia's development. The task of the proletariat would be to keep the bourgeoisie under the watchful eye of the masses so that it would complete the struggle against the old order, consolidate the freedoms which had been achieved and do nothing to harm the interests of the working class. Socialism still lay far in the future according to the Mensheviks. Its 'shining ideals' could not yet be achieved in a country that was only just beginning to overcome the backwardness in which despotism had left it. The European proletariat, on the other hand, had progressed much further and would have to show the way. It would take the united strength of the world proletariat to clear the path towards a socialist future for all humanity, but by taking a stand for

14. For the Menshevik position see the informative and well-documented memoirs of the leading Social Democrat of this period: I. Tsereteli, *Vospominaniya o russkoi revolyutsii* (Memoirs of the Russian Revolution) (Paris, 1963–4), vols. 1 and 2. Less informative is the Menshevik self-portrait by R.R. Abramovitch, *Die Sowjetrevolution* (Hannover, 1963).

freedom and democracy the Russian working class could make an invaluable contribution to the future of mankind.

For the time being, the Mensheviks were therefore convinced that everything that was historically possible and necessary was already being achieved through so-called *dvoevlastie* or 'dual power'. Menshevik plans for the evolution of society were completely satisfied by the new democracy and by the coexistence of Soviet and bourgeois government — workers' soviets, unions and factory committees functioning as organs of proletarian self-government alongside the institutions of the bourgeois state. The Menshevik wing of the Social Democratic Party saw itself as a bulwark of democracy and the rights of the people. It celebrated the eight-hour day, sang the 'Marseillaise' and looked forward with confidence to the day when the new freedoms would be confirmed in a parliamentary, democratic republic. Russia was on course.

In March 1917 this grand Menshevik design was still not seriously threatened by their Bolshevik rivals.[15] When the revolution erupted, very few members of Lenin's party were in Petrograd and those who were did not know for sure if the traditional formulas still applied. Should the evolving soviets be regarded as the 'revolutionary, democratic dictatorship of workers and peasants' which had figured on the Bolshevik agenda ever since 1905? What was the proper attitude to adopt towards the Provisional Government and the war? Did the fall of the Tsar signal the outbreak of the civil war, towards which Lenin had been inciting the proletariats of all the warring nations ever since 1914? Formerly banished party members were still returning in March to join the small Bolshevik faction, and their discussion of these issues produced a variety of responses. The Bolsheviks seemed to be preparing to form a radical minority, a left-wing opposition, in the soviets. Their chief endeavour would be to stoke the distrust already felt by the masses for the bourgeoisie and for those who had conceded power to it. This strategy was not altered until Lenin's return in April.[16]

---

15. For the Bolsheviks' lack of direction in March 1917 see Leonard Schapiro, *The Communist Party of the Soviet Union* (N.Y., 1960) and R.V. Daniels, *The Conscience of the Revolution. Communist Opposition in Soviet Russia* (1960). The discussion provoked by Burdzhalov in 1956 about Stalin's role (*Voprosy istorii* 1956, nos. 4 and 8) is not mentioned by Burdzhalov in his new book (see n.3). Burdzhalov was reprimanded at the time for his views.
16. W. Hahlweg, *Lenins Rückkehr nach Rußland* (Leiden, 1957), as well as the most recent Soviet presentation: A.V. Lukashev, 'Vosvrashchenie V.I. Lenina iz emigratsii v Rossiyu v aprele 1917g.', *Istoriya SSSR* (1963), no. 5, pp. 3–22.

It is important to realise that the liberal government and the parties in the soviets were united by one principal political factor in the spring of 1917: the war. Fragile, crisis democracy in Russia remained deeply immersed in the war and it was the war which brought about its downfall. As we have seen, the liberals participated in the Revolution only because they were convinced that the old regime was incapable of vigourously and successfully pursuing the war against the Central Powers. Over the years the liberals had grown accustomed to blaming tsarism for Russia's misadventures and defeats. Now that events had swept them into power, continued prosecution of the war remained a powerful impetus behind liberal policy. The liberals perceived continuation of the war as their real mandate and a source of political strength in the face of an internal lack of support which threatened to become permanent. Foreign Minister Milyukov was acutely aware of the situation. As a result of the demands posed by the war, the liberals seemed to have a chance to calm the violence of the revolution and to restore reasonableness and good judgment to revolutionary democracy. The alliance with England, France and soon the United States could be used to advantage in the internal struggle, as could the favour which liberal politicians hoped to curry in these countries thanks to their loyalty to the alliance.[17]

A good internal rationale therefore existed for continuing the war. Even apart from these reasons, the leading politicians in the Provisional Government had no incentive to favour a substantial revision of Russian policies towards the Entente. The liberals saw themselves as the champions of Russia's national interests and the guardians of an empire whose integrity was deeply threatened by revolutionary insurrection and a menacing military situation. The thought of negotiating a separate peace with the enemy from a position of weakness could not even be contemplated. If Russia was to survive the war with her status as a great power intact, Allied assistance would be essential. The liberals' confidence in final victory obviously received a powerful fillip when the United States entered the war. Woodrow Wilson's crusade for liberty and demo-

17. R.D. Warth, *The Allies and the Russian Revolution. From the Fall of the Monarchy to the Peace of Brest–Litovsk* (Durham, N.C., 1954), pp. 23ff., and the Soviet studies by A.E. Ioffe, *Russko-frantsuzskie otnosheniya v 1917g.* (Moscow, 1958); A.V. Ignat'ev, *Russko-angliiskie otnosheniya nakanune Oktyabr'skoi revolyutsii* (Moscow, 1966); V.S. Vasyukov, *Vneshnyaya politika Vremennogo pravitel'stva* (Moscow, 1966) as well as A.V. Ignat'ev in *Voprosy istorii* (1967), no. 3, pp. 3ff.

cracy offered the new Russia an honourable place in the ranks of free nations. The ideological view of the war which the President's messages carried to Europe could only be convincingly maintained thanks to the changes wrought by the Russian Revolution.[18] The low self-esteem of Russian liberals was enhanced by the sight of the great family of democratic nations at war against the forces of darkness in the form of 'Prussian autocracy'. The struggle against Teutonic militarism, German territorial ambitions and Prussian *Junkers* helped to reinforce the liberals' conviction that they stood on the side of liberty.

Nevertheless, the liberals did not push matters so far as to favour any tampering with the old tsarist war aims which the British and French had formally accepted. Like his European allies, Foreign Minister Milyukov assumed that Russia's security interests would be satisfied by means of sanctions and guarantees imposed on Germany in a peace treaty. Petrograd's desire to see a restored Poland subjected to Russian interests and its traditional wish to dominate the Straits found only muted expression in public, but this did not betoken any fundamental change in these aims.[19] Certain differences of opinion affected tactical nuances but not the substance of the liberal programme. In order to escape the opprobrium now attached on all sides to imperialism, the Petrograd cabinet couched its political ambitions in a democratic phraseology which could have been culled by this time from any mass circulation newspaper on either side of the front. Thus purified by lofty principles, Russian war aims emerged in acceptable form even without substantial amendment.

Pressure for change and for a clear break with tsarist foreign policy originated outside the government. The parties and movements represented in the soviets wished to see Russia's attitude towards the war re-expressed in terms of 'revolutionary democracy'. The Petrograd Soviet agreed to a continuation of the war on the side of the Allies, but it also insisted that Russia's commitment to the war had to be balanced by credible attempts to achieve peace.[20] Russian socialists could not bring themselves to speak of

18. Cf. L.I. Strakhovsky, *American Opinion about Russia, 1917–1920* (Toronto, 1961), Chr. Lasch, *The American Liberals and the Russian Revolution* (New York, 1962), and the approach taken by E. Hölzle in *Die Revolution der zweigeteilten Welt* (Hamburg, 1963), pp. 60ff.
19. See the documents in Browder and Kerensky, *The Provisional Government*, vol. II, pp. 1054ff.
20. D. Geyer, 'Die russischen Räte und die Friedensfrage', *Vierteljahreshefte für*

continuation of the war until final victory and the only policy which could be defended before the masses was the transformation of the scourge of war into a struggle for peace.

The victory of the Revolution made it easier for the parties in the Soviet to accept as inevitable the continuation of the war in the immediate future. Even those who had considered all talk of fighting to save the tsarist fatherland obsolete now agreed that democratic Russia, the homeland of the Revolution, had to be defended against German imperialism. It was no longer the despotic empire of the Tsar but the achievements of the Revolution, the victory of revolutionary democracy and the rights of the working masses which were being defended against an enemy to whom reactionary, imperialist and aggressive desires could easily be imputed. These were the sentiments evoked by a manifesto of the Petrograd Soviet issued on 14 (27) March and addressed the 'peoples of the world': 'We shall energetically defend our freedom against every reactionary attack from within or without. The Russian Revolution will not shrink before the bayonets of the conqueror and will not be subjugated by foreign armies.'[21] This decisive statement did not, however, exhaust the thoughts of the Soviet on this matter. These words appeared in the midst of revolutionary appeals intended first and foremost to prescribe standards of good conduct for the Russian government. The Soviet urged 'comrades, proletarians and working people of all countries' to seek peace not war. The struggle should be joined 'against the rapacious desires of governments in all countries'; the peoples of the world should take into their own hands the question of war or peace. The Soviet spoke out not in terms of an Allied victory over the Central Powers but in terms of victory for freedom and democracy around the world, of a restored and consolidated international solidarity and of a unified proletariat whose 'final victory' the Soviet applauded. The Petrograd Soviet had

---

Zeitgeschichte, Jg. 5 (1957), pp. 220–40. The desire for peace among the parties in the Soviet is misinterpreted when G. Wettig claims ('Die Rolle der Armee', pp. 246ff.) that the peace proposals were merely attempts to win over the masses 'to class war'. Wettig's contention that in reality the Soviet was concerned 'neither with propagating material measures [?] nor with satisfying the masses' demand for an end to the war' (p. 246) cannot be sustained. Artificial distinctions cannot be drawn between the role of principle and the role of strategy and tactical considerations in socialist agitation for a radically 'democratic peace among nations'. The terminology of class war is perfectly understandable as the traditional intellectual framework of pacifism, with roots reaching back to the prewar Socialist International and to the Zimmerwald movement.
21. Text in Hellmann, dtv 227/8, p. 181f.

clearly adopted the phraseology of the Zimmerwald movement. Peace without annexation or indemnities was the goal. The emotion and determination which ran through this manifesto derived from the confidence inspired by experiencing the Russian Revolution. The Soviet did not hesitate to point out to its 'proletarian brothers' behind enemy lines that with the overthrow of tsarism, 'the main pillar of world reaction', Germany's most important reason for pursuing the war had been eliminated. The 'Asiatic despotism' which formerly had menaced liberty and civilisation existed no more. A challenge was therefore flung down to the German proletariat to emulate its Russian comrades: 'Free yourselves from the yoke of your semi-autocratic regime, as the Russian people have freed themselves from tsarist autocracy. Refuse to become a tool for conquest and violence in the hands of kings, Junkers and bankers.' The Russian example was recommended not only for the Germans but for all nationalities. According to the manifesto, the mighty voice of the Russian people was now making itself felt in foreign affairs and the masses were determined to spare no effort to overturn the policy of conquest practised by their own ruling class. It remained for the peoples of Europe to join in 'this decisive battle for peace'. In a conversation with English and French socialists, Kerensky further clarified the views of the Soviet: 'We expect you to exercise the same decisive influence over the other classes in your countries that we have exercised over our own bourgeoisie which now renounces all imperialist intentions.'[22] Evidently the Russians did not suffer from a lack of self-confidence. So far as they were concerned, the watchdog capacity which the soviets claimed to exercise over the Provincial Government could serve as a model for other countries as well.

At the end of March an agreement had in fact been reached within the framework of 'dual power' which made it possible to arrive, at least verbally, at a consensus view of the war.[23] The Soviet was compelled daily to justify its condominium with the government and was therefore most anxious to extract binding guarantees from the cabinet that Russian policy was now free of all imperialistic tendencies, that a democratic peace was being sought and that all territorial was aims had been renounced. The Soviet leadership also insisted on negotiating a statement intended to drape the foreign

22. *Krasnyi Arkhiv* XV, pp. 62ff.
23. For the evolution of the negotiations see I. Tseretelli, *Vospominaniya*, vol. I, pp. 59ff.

policy of the new Russia in democratic trappings.

The government, on the other hand, wished to mollify the vehemence of the peace campaign waged in the soviets and to secure socialist support for a continuation of the war. With Soviet backing for the government, the Minister of War hoped that 'new enthusiasm for the defence of the country' could be instilled in the troops. Although the Soviet could afford to run the risk of open conflict within the dual power system, the government could not and it was therefore constrained to agree to concessions and a verbal compromise. In the end, only the Foreign Minister was reluctant to accept them. After protracted negotiations a declaration was issued on 27 March by which the government apparently satisfied the wishes of Soviet spokesmen:

> The goal of free Russia is not rule over other peoples, not the pillage of their national wealth nor forced annexation of foreign territory but a lasting peace on the basis of the self-determination of peoples. The Russian people does not wish to expand its external power at the cost of other peoples and is not interested in enslaving or denigrating others. . . .[24]

Thanks to the Soviet, government policy was apparently now bound by the principles of self-determination and no annexation. At the same time, the United States was trying to create an ideological consensus within the Entente based on these same precepts. The Americans hoped that this would create a climate in which democracy would flourish long after peace had been declared. The language employed by the Russian and American governments had thus converged, though there is no way of knowing if this apparent understanding could have borne the stresses and strains of reality. It is possible that this apparent identity of views was misleading, that continuing conflicts of interest were simply camouflaged and not resolved. In any case, the parties within the Soviet promised to remain vigilant and to guard against any reversion on the part of the government to the war aims of the old regime. Distrust of bourgeois proclivities to imperialism remained strong.

In the meantime, the accord was imperilled not by the government but by a third party. Even before a statement issued by

24. For the text of the government declaration see Golder, *Documents in Russian History*, pp. 329ff.

Foreign Minister Milyukov spread like wildfire, upsetting the internal truce and provoking the first crisis of dual power,[25] Lenin returned to Petrograd on 3 (16) April with the assistance of the German government and began flatly to contradict the official Soviet view of the situation. True, Lenin also interpreted events in Russia as a bourgeois revolution. But since soviet democracy had renounced power and delegated it to a bourgeois government, the war remained an imperialist war of conquest in Lenin's eyes. While still in Zurich Lenin had staked out his position in his 'Letters from Afar' which stood in marked contrast to the views of those in Petrograd who supported 'dual power'. The Russian bourgeoisie was still waging the same imperialist war it had pursued under the Tsar, Lenin claimed, and no reason therefore existed to encourage the people to support the Provisional Government and defend the motherland. Moreover this government, bound hand and foot by English and French capital, was essentially incapable of seeking any other kind of peace than an aggressive, imperialist peace. Lenin insisted that claims that this 'government by capital' could cease acting in an imperialist fashion were a pernicious illusion and a betrayal of the true interests of the working masses. Without the defeat of capital and the collapse of bourgeois government, a genuinely democratic peace could never be achieved.

The conclusions which Lenin drew from this analysis were expressed forcefully in his renowned 'April Theses': to strive for peace meant to struggle against the Provisional Government, to strip power away from the bourgeoisie and to turn it over to the people — 'into the hands of the proletariat and the poorest sections of the peasantry'.[26] The revolution was far from over and the Bolsheviks should do all they could to continue it. The new Bolshevik slogan, 'all power to the soviets', was the logical result. Lenin's declaration of war on the Provisional Government amounted to a declaration of war on those deputies in the soviets who wished to continue supporting the government. Plekhanov was not far off the mark when he declared that Lenin's theses had planted 'the banner of civil war' in the midst of revolutionary democracy.[27] Before the year was

25. See the following chapter for the April Crisis.
26. Lenin, 'Letters from Afar' in *Collected Works*, (Moscow, 1962), vol. 23, pp. 309ff.
27. Lenin's 'April Theses: The Tasks of the Proletariat in the Present Revolution' (*Pravda* no. 26, 7 April 1917) in *Collected Works* (Moscow, 1962), vol. 24, pp. 21–5. For the pre-history of the theses see G.N. Golikov and Yu.S. Tokarev in *Voprosy*

out the hastily improvised democracy of the February Revolution had been overwhelmed, not only by the pressures of the continuing World War, but also by the <u>civil war which now ensued</u>.[28]

istorii (1967), no. 4, pp. 3–20. For the discussions about Lenin's programme within the Bolshevik party see Schapiro, *The Communist Party* and Daniels, *The Conscience of the Revolution*.

28. Plekhanov's position on the April Theses (according to *Edinstvo*, no. 9–11, 9–12 April 1917) can be found in G.V. Plekhanov, *God na rodine. Polnoe sobranie statei i rechei 1917–1918gg.* (Paris, 1921), vol. 1, pp. 19ff.

7

The Erosion of Dual Power

Like every great scheme which is intended to be put into practice, Lenin's revolutionary theory was marvellous in its simplicity. Written in very closely argued logic, his 'April Theses' cast a new light on the present and the future of the Russian Revolution.[1] By analysing what had already occurred, Lenin arrived at his convictions as to what should happen next. The party's programme and goals were seen as a product of necessity; revolutionary politics would do what objectively had to be done. The truth as propagated by Lenin was of course highly partisan, but this very fact intensified the light which it shed and increased its political effectiveness. Little changes if reality is not approached from a particular point of view.

Lenin's views based on the following argument: The February Revolution was only the *first* stage in the Russian Revolution. It had swept the bourgeoisie into power, created government by capitalists, and made Russia 'the freest of all the belligerent countries'. The bourgeoisie had been able to seize power precisely because the proletariat was not yet sufficiently class conscious or well organised. The proletarian masses, which had just awakened to political life, continued to trust blindly in capitalist government. The soviets, the most precious fruit of the revolution, were dominated by petty bourgeois, opportunist elements which had succumbed to the influence of the bourgeoisie and which helped to maintain its hold over the proletariat. The Bolshevik party, not more than a weak minority at the present time, would have to adapt to these conditions. Its tactics would be to enlighten the masses, criticise error and eliminate false consciousness.

According to Lenin, the Bolsheviks would have to emphasise a number of points. Firstly, the war remained what it always had

---

1. Cf. chapter 6, n.7.

been: an imperialist was of aggression. The Provisional Government represented government by capital and was therefore necessarily imperialist. All assurances that it had renounced annexationist claims were lies. The Provisional Government was 'the worst enemy of peace and socialism'. It could not possibly conclude a genuinely democratic peace because such a peace presupposes the fall of capital. Secondly, since this was an imperialist war, talk of revolutionary defence of the motherland was absurd. Even the smallest concession on this point was inadmissible. The war would only become revolutionary when power had been stripped from the bourgeoisie and transferred 'into the hands of the proletariat and the poorest sections of the peasants aligned with the proletariat'. Only then would 'revolutionary defence of the fatherland' cease to be a hypocritical slogan. Thirdly, the transfer of all state power into the hands of the proletariat and the poorest peasantry would constitute 'the *second* stage of the revolution'. The only possible form of revolutionary government would be soviets of workers' deputies. Since these soviets already existed, Russia had already traversed the phase of parliamentary republicanism and pleas for such a republic were a step backwards. Progress on the other hand entailed a struggle for a soviet republic of workers', rural labourers' and peasants' deputies and the transition to a 'commune state'.

The circumstances in which these ideas were advanced must also be considered. Lenin's thought was dynamic, not static, for he saw the Revolution as a continuing process. The old formulas 'are already antiquated' Lenin wrote in April.[2] 'In real life things have *already* turned out *differently*; there has been an . . . unprecedented *interlacing*' of the dictatorship of the bourgeoisie, in the form of the Provisional Government, and the dictatorship of peasants and pro-letarians, in the form of soviets of workers', soldiers' and peasants' deputies. Both existed side by side and were interconnected because most of the political forces in the soviets which supported a revolutionary, democratic dictatorship of workers and peasants had voluntarily abandoned power to the bourgeoisie. According to Lenin, this situation forced the Bolsheviks to change their strategy:

> The person who *now* speaks [as the Bolsheviks had done ever since 1905] of a 'revolutionary-democratic dictatorship of the proletariat and the peasantry' is behind the times, consequently, he has in effect gone *over* to

2. Lenin, 'Letters on Tactics' in *Collected Works* (Moscow, 1962), vol. 24, pp. 42–54.

the petty bourgeoisie; the person should be consigned to the archive of 'Bolshevik' pre-revolutionary antiques.

This form of dictatorship had already been attained in Russia, according to Lenin, as part of 'dual power'. It was now a question of forging beyond this stage, of separating the proletarian, 'Communist', 'internationalist' elements from the petty bourgeois elements and marshalling the strength of those who were in favour of 'moving towards the commune'.

By the 'commune' Lenin did not then mean merely the soviets in their present form, dominated by Socialist Revolutionaries and Menshevik Social Democrats, the 'ideologues of the petty bourgeois masses'. What Lenin wished instead was to remould the soviets themselves, to purge them of opportunist and petty bourgeois influence so that they would be able to carry out the functions of the commune, a new and revolutionary kind of state:

> We need a revolutionary *government*; we need (for a certain transitional period) a *state*. That is what distinguishes us from the anarchists. . . . We need a state. But *not* the kind the bourgeoisie needs with organs of government . . . separate from and opposed to the people. All bourgeois revolutions merely perfected *this* state machine, merely transferred *it* from the hands of one party to those of another. The proletariat, on the other hand, if it wants to proceed further, must 'smash', to use Marx's expression, this 'ready-made' state machine and substitute a new one for it by *merging the police force, the army and the bureaucracy with the entire armed people. . . . The proletariat must organise and arm all* the poor, exploited sections of the population in order that they *themselves* should take the organs of state power directly into their own hands, in order that *they themselves should constitute* these organs of power.[3]

Here Lenin's argument referred back to history. Only the Paris Commune, he explained, ever succeeded in creating this kind of government. Marx had already recognised in the Paris Commune a political structure 'under which the economic liberation of work' could occur. According to Lenin, this kind of state already existed in embryonic form and for the first time in Russia in the workers' soviets of 1905. Now, in 1917, the groundwork for the commune state was being laid by the new soviets. Lenin assumed that the

---

3. 'Letters from Afar III' (11/24 March 1917) in *Collected Works* (Moscow, 1962), vol. 23, pp. 325ff. Cf. K. Meschkat, *Die Pariser Kommune von 1871 im Spiegel der sowjetischen Geschichtsschreibung* (Berlin, 1965), pp. 65ff.

commune would emerge and destroy the old state machine when the soviets had been purged of opportunist and petty bourgeois elements and all power had been transferred to the thus purified soviets. This was at the heart of the Bolsheviks cry, 'all power to the soviets!'. When speaking of the 'commune' Lenin meant the transitional stage between capitalism and socialism.

The plan which the Bolsheviks elaborated from these principles avoided any appearance of aiming at the *violent* overthrow of the Provisional Government and of the bourgeoisie. The soviets, not the Bolshevik party, were supposed to prepare to seize power. This was primarily a question of tactics. In the spring of 1917, nothing could be done without the approval of the soviets. Calls for rebellion or civil war would have isolated the Bolsheviks in a minority position. They therefore attempted to dominate the soviets, not quit them. Lenin never considered an attempt to seize power without the support of a majority of the proletarian and semi-proletarian masses: 'We are not Blanquists, we do not stand for the seizure of power by a minority.'[4] What Lenin did want at this time was to revolutionise the soviets, to isolate and discredit their leadership and win mass support for the revolutionary policies of his party. Many of Lenin's opponents discerned a conspiratorial, Blanquist core to Bolshevik policies, but this stemmed primarily from the Bolsheviks' refusal to feel bound by the rules of the crisis democracy in their struggle for majority support.

Every demand of Bolshevik agitators contrasted sharply with the policies which other parties in the soviets had pursued since March 1917. The Bolsheviks demanded that the government immediately propose a general end to the war and they called on the armies at the front to fraternise with the enemy. The other parties had committed themselves to continuing the war in collaboration with the government and the Allies. Since nothing concrete could be undertaken, they had to content themselves with long-winded declarations of their desire for peace. The Bolsheviks insisted that the army be disbanded and the general population armed, while the other parties felt compelled to assist the government in reversing the radical democratisation of the army and in restoring the authority of the officer corps. The troops had to prepare for battle — not only defensive operations but also the new offensive which the Allies were expecting from democratic Russia.

4. 'The Dual Power' (9 April 1917) in *Collected Works*, vol. 24, p. 40.

Besides questions of war and peace, Bolshevik plans for agriculture proved to be especially effective at inching the Russian Revolution towards its 'second stage'.[5] The Bolsheviks demanded that the landowning nobility be immediately dispossessed and that all land be nationalised and placed under the authority of the soviets of peasants' and agricultural labourers' deputies. In the midst of war the other parties could not even consider such a radical solution to the agrarian question. It might well have choked off the flow of supplies to the army, which were already at dangerously low levels. The ranks of the army would have been further decimated if even more peasants set off home in order to be present for the redistribution of the land. For these reasons, the other parties in the soviets were compelled to insist stubbornly that only the projected Constituent Assembly could decide on land reform. Until such times, only preparatory measures could be undertaken and statistics garnered on the land available for redistribution. The most that could be done was to determine the utilisation of state land.

Bolshevik agitation regarding the nationalities was no less provocative.[6] Lenin's party insisted that the non-Russian peoples should be granted the fullest possible right to self-determination — even if this resulted in outright separation (for instance in the case of the Ukraine or the Caucasus). The other parties could not countenance any dismemberment of the Empire. Although movements of national autonomy (with the exception of the Poles) were demanding only national independence within the framework of a federation, the other socialist parties tried to prevent them from proceeding on their own with autonomy. The government was forced to insist vigorously on the integrity of the central administration because any restructuring would have had consequences that could not be foreseen or justified from a military and economic point of view. If an autonomous Ukrainian republic had taken over the administration of southern industry, the central government in Petrograd would have been inundated with new problems. This explains the conflict which actually did erupt between Petrograd and

5. See S. Dubrowski, *Die Bauernbewegung in der russischen Revolution 1917* (Berlin, 1929). For the documents see Browder and Kerensky, *The Provisional Government*, vol. 2, pp. 523ff. and *Krest'yanskoe dvizhenie v 1917 godu*, (Tsentrarkhiv, Moscow–Leningrad, 1927).
6. The most important work is by R. Pipes, *The Formation of the Soviet Union. Communism and Nationalism 1917–1923*, 2nd revised edn. (Cambridge, Mass., 1964), pp. 50ff.

Kiev, soon embroiling the non-Bolshevik parties in the soviets.[7] According to them, all long-term decisions on the nationalities question (which had become highly explosive after the February Revolution) would also have to be referred to the Constituent Assembly. Only in the case of Poland, now occupied by the enemy, did the government agree under pressure from the Allies and the Petrograd Soveit to create an independent state bound to Russia by a 'free military union'.[8] Finland was allowed to recover its former autonomy but was not permitted to leave the Empire; nor was the Russian Governor-General withdrawn.[9]

The Bolsheviks also proposed revolutionary alternatives to the economic policies of the coalition government.[10] Lenin's party demanded that the entire banking system be nationalised and administered by workers' soviets. The other parties found their hands tied by the fact that such a step would likely have provoked the final collapse of the shaky financial system. With its links to Allied capital markets, the financial sector formed the foundation of the war effort. Inflation was running high and the system was barely able to keep industry turning over as things were. The Bolsheviks demanded that control over industrial production and the distribution of goods be transferred to the workers' soviets. this reflected the demands of many union organisations and especially the attempts of the factory committees, which had been constituted in all industries after the February Revolution, to extend worker self-

---

7. For the Ukranian problem see (besides Pipes, pp. 53ff), the study by J.S. Reshetar, *The Ukranian Revolution 1917–1921* (Princeton, N.J., 1952). Also D. Geyer, 'Die Ukraine im Jahre 1917', *Geschichte in Wissenschaft und Unterricht* 8 (Jg. 1957), pp. 670–87.

8. For the text of the Provisional Government's address on Poland on 16 March 1917 see Browder and Kerensky, *The Provisional Government*, vol. I, pp. 320ff.; *Dokumenty i materialy po istorii sovetsko-polskikh otnoshenii* (Moscow, 1963), vol. I; *Materialy archiwalne do historii stosunków Polskich-Radzieckich* (Warsaw, 1957), vol. I. For studies see T. Komarnicki, *Re-birth of the Polish Republic. A Study in the Diplomatic History of Europe 1914–1920* (London, 1957), W. Conze, *Polnische Nation und deutsche Politik im ersten Weltkrieg* (Cologne, 1958).

9. C. Jay Smith, *Finland and the Russian Revolution, 1917–1922* (University of Georgia Press, 1958), pp. 12ff.; J.H. Hudgson, *Communism in Finland. A History and Interpretation* (Princeton, N.J., 1967), and the documents in Browder and Kerensky, *The Provisional Government*, vol. I, pp. 334ff.

10. For what follows see R. Lorenz, 'Zur Industriepolitik der Provisorischen Regierung', *Jahrbücher für Geschichte Osteuropas* 14 (1966), pp. 36ff. and, from the Soviet Union, P.V. Volobuev, *Ekonomicheskaya politika Vremennogo pravitel'stva* (The Economic policies of the Provisional Government) (Moscow, 1962). Documents in Browder and Kerensky, *The Provisional Government*, vol. I, pp. 479ff.; *Ekonomicheskoe polozhenie Rossii nakanune Velikoi Oktyabr'skoi Sotsialicheskoi Revolyutsii* (Russia's economic position on the eve of the October Revolution) (Moscow, 1957), vols. 1 and 2.

management to factory level. The other parties involved in 'dual power' were forced to be extremely cautious in this regard too because factory owners had only one effective response to such attempts; namely to close the factories and lock the workers out. Factory owners could do this all the more easily in that inflation had cut deeply into income and many branches of industry were barely making a profit. However, politicians concerned primarily with steering Russia safely through the war and the period of crisis could not permit industrial shut-downs. Entrepreneurial associations even succeeded in blocking attempts to match the Germans and extend state monopolies in order to improve the organisation of wartime production. In addition, the grain monopoly which was introduced to force goods onto the market could not be fully implemented.

In all of this one can see the embarrassing position in which the parties of 'revolutionary democracy' found themselves. Both the Mensheviks and Socialist Revolutionaries suffered fateful consequences as a result of the constraints imposed on them by participation in a government that was determined to pursue the war. Their freedom of action was severely curtailed and they were compelled in almost all important questions that aroused the passion of the masses to counsel moderation, patience and reasonableness — virtues of limited attractiveness in times of unrest and mass upheaval. The Mensheviks and SRs had to maintain their credibility as pillars of the state if they did not wish to abandon the new democracy to the ruling liberals or even to generals who had the ear of ministers in Petrograd and were offering to dispel the spectre of revolution and restore order. They were haunted by the danger of a military dictatorship, of 'counter-revolution', and not without reason. At the same time, they came under pressure from those whom they were supposed to be representing in the soviets: workers, who wished to govern rather than be governed; soldiers, reluctant to relinquish their freedoms before renewed military discipline and war-weary elements of the population who could not discern much sign of the vaunted revolution in the policies pursued by the government. In addition, the Mensheviks and SRs faced a determined Bolshevik challenge and all-out agitation in the factories and the barracks, at the front and behind the lines, to underscore the discrepancy between reality and the claims of the Soviet leadership.

As time progressed, the Bolsheviks found it ever easier to find an audience for their complaints. The government, they argued, was incapable of concluding peace; the land would remain the property

91

of the large landowners; the government was a suppressive tool of the class enemy that merely mouthed revolutionary phrases suggested by SRs and Menshevik opportunists — it was a dishonest government, supported by people claiming to be socialists but really working to conceal their treachery because they had become lackeys of the bourgeoisie and were betraying the revolution to its counter-revolutionary enemies. In the long run, the majority parties could do little to refute these charges. Loss of authority could not be prevented when the achievements of the revolution had to be rescinded, despite assurances that they were being valiantly defended, when nothing developed from all the fine talk in the Soviet. These paradoxes made the policies of the Mensheviks and SRs seem confused and diffuse, their rhetoric hollow. Their reserves of strength were steadily worn away. The non-Bolshevik socialists never succeeded in resolving their central dilemma: how simultaneously to maintain authority over the masses and influence over the government. In the end both were lost, and a path was cleared for the Bolsheviks to step into the breach.

How quickly the majority in the Soviet could lose its hold over the masses became evident before the end of April.[11] In Petrograd and elsewhere, large May Day demonstrations (held on 18 April) went far beyond the mere chanting of trade union slogans. Instead of rejoicing in the new age which the revolution had introduced, the crowds seemed determine to practise permanent protest in the streets and to transform the celebrations into bitter demonstrations against the government. Down with the war! Down with (Foreign Minister) Milyukov! Long live democratic peace without annexations or indemnities! Hundreds of thousands of workers and soldiers chanted slogans such as these in front of government offices. The immediate source of the unrest was a note from Milyukov to the Allied governments which had become known to the public. In it Milyukov spoke of a victorious peace, of conscienciously fulfilling the treaties that had been ratified, of the 'guarantees and sanctions' which would be necessary to lay the groundwork for a lasting peace.[12] The Foreign Minister's words implied nothing which could

11. For the April crisis see I.G. Tsereteli, *Vospominaniya o fevral'skoi revolyutsii* vol. I, pp. 77ff.; Browder and Kerensky, *The Provisional Government*, vol. III, pp. 1236ff.; 'Revolyutsionnoe dvizhenie v Rossii v aprele' in *Velikaya Oktyabr'skaya Sotsialisticheskaya Revolyutsiya. Dokumenty i materialy* (Moscow, 1958); also: I.I. Mints, 'Pervyi krizis vlasti v aprele' in *Voprosy istorii* (1967), no. 1, pp. 3–26.

12. For the text of Milyukov's note see Browder and Kerensky, *The Provisional Government*, vol. II, p. 1098; see also R.D. Warth, *The Allies and the Russian*

not be deduced from policies which the Soviet had approved, but this clear statement of the facts focused attention on matters customarily enveloped in a fog of revolutionary phraseology. The folly of stating the truth in public quickly became apparent. The Bolsheviks did their best to spread the news and to elaborate on the diplomatic note. This provided a testing ground for the effectiveness of their public agitation. For tactical reasons, they refrained from calls to overthrow the government and confined themselves to voicing the general sense of dissatisfaction and distrust. They succeeded in resisting the temptation to urge the common people into taking extreme action.

The demonstrations and parades continued until 21 April and they were certainly no less painful for the socialist politicians than for the government. If the socialists did not want to leave the government and cede power to the generals, they would have to demonstrate their capabilities and prove again that they had the government as firmly under control as they had always claimed. Bland assurances and mild criticism of Milyukov would not suffice.[13] The discredited system of 'dual power' had to be strengthened and renewed. Efforts in this direction finally succeeded in putting an end to the so-called 'April Crisis' which had eventually spread even to the ranks of the government.

At the end of April, Minister of War Guchkov resigned in a storm of protest. He complained that his ministry could do nothing to halt the massive destruction of the Russian army and navy. With the very existence of the nation at stake, he was no longer prepared to be held responsible. Guchkov's resignation was a direct result of the plight in which the army found itself.[14] Commanding officers declared that their orders were being ignored and that the military operations which the Allies had been promised could not be undertaken. Soldiers habitually refused to obey orders from the military command and voted to rescind them. The entreaties of officers could not prevent the merits of every order being debated at endless

---

Revolution (1954), pp. 45ff., V.S. Vasyukov, *Vneshnyaya Politika*, pp. 123ff.

13. Browder and Kerensky, *The Provisional Government*, vol. II, p. 1100, Tsereteli, *Vospominaniya*, vol. I, pp. 102ff.

14. See Wettig, 'Die Rolle der Armee', pp. 288ff.; also L. Graf Spannocchi, *Das Ende des Kaiserlich-Russischen Heeres* (Vienna–Leipzig, 1932). Documents in Browder and Kerensky, *The Provisional Government*, vol. II, pp. 845ff., *Razlozhenie armii v 1917g.* Tsentrarkhiv (Moscow–Leningrad, 1925) (= *1917 g. v dokumentakh i materialakh*).

company meetings. The complaints emanating from the army command amounted to an undisguised attack on the democratisation process which the Petrograd Soviet had undertaken with its famous Order No. 1 and which could no longer be rescinded. The April Crisis developed into a cabinet crisis.

Protracted negotiations between the government and the executive committee of the Soviet led to a momentous restructuring of the cabinet on 5 May. Milyukov was dismissed and Kerensky took over the War Ministry. Two more Socialist Revolutionaries, a Popular Socialist and two Mensheviks (including Tseretelli who was already chairman of the Soviet executive Committee and now became Minister of Posts) entered the government. In this way a formal coalition was created between 'bourgeois democracy' and 'revolutionary democracy'. Socialist took over such key ministries as war, justice, agriculture, labour and food.[15]

One might be tempted to see participation in the government by leading figures from the Soviet as an appropriate solution to the crisis. Everything had to be undertaken to reduce the structural weaknesses inherent in the system of dual power. The war cabinets in London and Paris had also been extended under the *'union sacrée'* to include 'red' ministers and were structured very similarly. The tensions between the government and the Soviet would apparently now be shifted from the liaison commissions to the coalition cabinet. Since both sides shared responsibility, this seemed likely to moderate conflict and mollify the aroused masses. Liberals still outnumbered socialists in the coalition government, and they hoped that the decline in the authority of the state could more easily be halted if the people responsible for the revolution were placed in a position where they had to master the forces it unleashed. The soviet leadership also detected advantages in the coalition. They could claim that the permanent presence of socialist ministers guaranteed that revolutionaries had now acquired firm control over the state. Soviet democracy was no longer on the outside looking in; the will of the people had finally entered important ministries and the cabinet. It remained to be seen whether more had been done than simply to assuage the deep-seated scepticism of the people.[16]

Very soon the truth of the old Russian saying that power is a burden and a sister to sorrow was once again manifested. Not all

15. M. Ferro, *La révolution de 1917*, pp. 324ff.
16. Cf. Tsereteli, *Vospominaniya*, vol. I, pp. 138ff., Browder and Kerensky, *The Provisional Government*, vol. III, pp. 1286ff.

those who participated in the government were fired with the zealous feeling that their official duties were the mission of a lifetime or imagined, like Kerensky, that they had been summoned to be Russia's guide and saviour. The government's declarations were laced, to be sure, with more revolutionary pathos than ever before, and there were no shortage of touching assurances and solemn affirmations that all the principles were being adhered to. However, such verbal radicalism could not long cloak the helplessness of the socialists or compensate for the fact that they had lost what would now be called political visibility in a coalition which tended to obfuscate their presence. Meanwhile, the peasant masses, anxious to proceed on their own with land redistribution, were no more dissuaded by Chernov, the Socialist Revolutionary Minister of Agriculture, than they had been by his predecessor. Indeed, the presence of such a prominent comrade in the ministry seemed to demonstrate convincingly that the Socialist Revolutionaries could not deliver on their party programme. The Constituent Assembly still seemed far in the future; elections, it was said, would be held in September. The socialist Minister of Food proved unable to halt the steep rise in prices or alleviate the severe food shortages. What is more, he now bore the blame for the crisis. The Menshevik Minister of Labour experienced no greater success in reconciling his class brethren in the factories to their misery. He too of course was held completely responsible for the workers' grievances. Socialist ministers were now forced by the official positions they held in the government to pursue rigid policies. The fact that ministers always run the risk of sharing the fate of any group they support was enough to discourage any startling attempts at reform. Unable to elaborate policies which differed substantially from those of their bourgeois colleagues, the socialists could no longer distance themselves from the prevailing conditions in Russia. They had even become ultimately responsible for them.

The political situation was dominated by one unfortunate fact. The whole *raison d'être* of the coalition was the war — continuing the war, restoring the army's battle-readiness and preparing for a summer offensive. The driving force within the cabinet was Kerensky, the Minister of War. He proved to be a tribune without staying power, a virtuoso of feigned passion and a prisoner of his own brilliant rhetoric. As soon as the grand spectacle came to an end, his charisma evaporated. The problems of these confused, terrible times can be seen in the success which Kerensky enjoyed for several weeks in reducing all politics to the gestures of an anointed leader, in mollifying the fears of the bourgeoisie by adopting the pose of the passionate patriot and in convincing the masses by means of his hectic schedule that the flame was still alight so long as he was working for revolution, democracy and freedom. Apart from this remarkable man, much of the rest of the government coalition also became convinced that they were compelled to make a supreme effort on which the success or failure of Russia's fragile democracy would depend.[17]

Contrary to all military logic, an offensive was therefore ordered at the end of June. The new government wished to demonstrate Russia's ability to continue as a partner in the war and to restore in the Allied capitals the confidence which it itself had lost in the hope that aid shipments to Russia would be restored to their previous levels. The world be shown that democratic Russia had not succumbed to chaos and anarchy. The coalition also hoped that even modest, partial successes in the war would have a salutary effect within Russia. Confidence would be restored and renewed patriotism and pride would counteract the mounting signs of crisis and dissolution. Revolutionary energy which could not be released within Russia could be offered a foreign outlet. The military preparations were accompanied of course by eloquent assurances that the government's unshakable hope was for a democratic peace.[18] The radical–democratic pacifism which still flourished in the soviets was not suppressed but was encouraged to direct its attention outwards towards other governments. Opposition voices that could have upset the plans of the Minister of War were preoccupied with preparations for the socialist peace conference in Stockholm which proceeded amidst a barrage of propaganda. Ever since the April Days, the Soviet leadership had espoused the Stockholm initiative as a welcome addition to its own peace manifestoes, but now Stockholm became a kind of alibi behind which one could hide when asked what was being done for peace as the war continued to rage.[19]

The July offensive turned out to be the last, convulsive outpouring of all the remaining energy in the regime, a crucial test of the emergency coalition. The enterprise was a complete disaster and

17. Browder and Kerensky, *The Provisional Government*, vol. II, pp. 921ff.
18. For the July offensive see: Wettig, 'Die Rolle der Armee', pp. 314ff., Tsereteli, *Vospominaniya*, vol. II, pp. 7ff.
19. Tsereteli, *Vospominaniya*, vol. I, pp. 169ff. Cf. D. Geyer, 'Die Russischen Räte und die Friedensfrage', pp. 220ff.

provided within a few days conclusive evidence of Russia's impotence. The effects were devastating. Russian democracy was incapable of making war, but it was also incapable of making peace. The Allies stubbornly refused the coalition government's request that war aims be reviewed and a joint peace proposal offered.[20] No comfort could be derived from the likely results of the socialist conference in Stockholm. It had long been clear that the peace initiative would flounder on the hostilities which the war had engendered in the parties towards the old International. In addition, the governments of England and France did all they could to disavow the conference. At the meeting itself, squabbles broke out even during the preliminary negotiations and long before the central issues could be addressed.[21] Finally, the coalition government in Petrograd collapsed when liberal ministers, with Premier Lvov at their head, resigned in the wake of arguments about Ukrainian autonomy. 'Dual power', that fine fiction of improvised democracy, had come to an end.[22]

Kerensky became the new Prime Minister. In the style of a plebiscitary dictator without a democratic mandate, he attempted a balancing act over the raging chaos below. First he had to fend off the danger posed by those who offered a revolutionary alternative. With Russia in crisis, the Bolsheviks had the wind in their sails. Early in July they took to the streets of Petrograd with armed demonstrations directed against the government — a mass review of their own supporters which threatened to turn into an insurrection that the party could not control. Lenin was testing the possibility of such an insurrection, but did not dare proceed with it in the teeth of opposition from the Soviet.[23] The government responded to the so-called July *putsch* with police measures and court actions which greatly damaged Bolshevik organisation but did little to reduce mounting Bolshevik influence in the army and among the proletariat. Charges that Lenin's party had accepted money from the Germans and had been bought off by Russia's foes caused a stir, but most workers and soldiers lent little credence to the thesis that

20. R.D. Warth, *The Allies and the Russian Revolution*, p. 149.
21. H. Meynell, 'The Stockholm Conference of 1917', *International Review of Social History* V (1960), pp. 1–25, 202–25.
22. Tsereteli, *Vospominaniya* vol. II, pp. 133ff., Browder and Kerensky, *The Provisional Government*, vol. III, pp. 1382ff.
23. On the July Crisis see O.N. Znamenskii, *Iyul'skii krizis 1917g.* (Moscow–Leningrad, 1964); Browder and Kerensky, vol. III, pp. 1335ff.; Tsereteli pp. 259ff., *Revolyutsionnoe dvizhenie v Rossii v iyule. Iyul'skii krizis* (Moscow, 1959).

Lenin was really a German agent leading a 'germano–bolshevik plot'. Although Lenin did not go to court, this attempt at character assassination had little effect in the long run.[24] When the supreme commander, General Kornilov, tried to overthrow Kerensky in a military coup at the end of August,[25] the Bosheviks demonstrated that they were already the only unified, effective force within the revolutionary democracy. The crisis in Russia had become a permanent one and the time was ripe for Lenin to put insurrection and a *coup d'état* on the Bolshevik agenda.

24. Cf. Chapter 5, n.4, as well as Tsereteli, pp. 332ff.
25. For the Kornilov revolt see A. Ascher, 'The Kornilov Affair', *The Russian Review*, vol. 12 (1953), pp. 235–52. Also, the documents in Browder and Kerensky, *The Provisional Government*, vol. III, pp. 1527ff. and the Soviet documentation in the series, *Velikaya Oktyabr'skaya Sotsialisticheskaya Revolyutsiya. Dokumenty i materialy: Revolyutsionnoe dvizhenie v Rossii v avguste 1917g. Razgrom Kornilovskogo myatezha* (Moscow, 1959), *Revolyutsionnoe dvizhenie v Rossii v sentyabre 1917g. Obshchenatsional'nyi krizis* (Moscow, 1961).

8

Insurrection and the Seizure of Power

The event to which we now turn our attention bears many names, none of which quite does it justice: *coup d'état*, uprising, insurrection, or 'Great Socialist October Revolution'; a minority conspiracy or 'Ten Days That Shook the World'; *action directe* on the part of a few resolute figures or 'Red October', a turning-point in world history. Opinions vary enormously and the nuances, of which history itself is made, are forever fascinating. The questions extend far beyond the plain facts which might appear to reveal 'what really happened'. This would probably not be so if these events could be reduced to a *putsch*, to an occurence so simple that one could say: 'The Bolsheviks did not seize power. They picked it up.'[1] History was in the making, and this explains perhaps why we can no longer separate the consequences of the events from the events themselves.

Despite all the controversy, unanimity probably reigns with respect to at least one point: the change of government in October was the result of an insurrection, of violent action aimed at overthrowing the Provisional Government with the armed assistance of the Petrograd garrison, the Baltic fleet and the working class, organised and steered by the Bolshevik party. However, if a single step is taken beyond this simple statement matters are no longer so clear. Even the term 'insurrection' is questionable, for no description is possible that does not seem to imply a value judgement. The implications of the word 'insurrection' are immediately questioned and so unanimity evaporates.

1. A.B. Ulam, *Lenin and the Bolsheviks: The Intellectual and the Political History of the Triumph of Communism in Russia* (London, 1966), p. 314; a detailed description of events to date in S. Melgunov, *Kak bol'sheviki zakhvatili vlast': Oktyabr'skii perevorot 1917 goda* (How the Bolsheviks seized power: the October Revolution 1917) (Paris, 1953); more recently, R.V. Daniels, *Red October. The Bolshevik Revolution of 1917* (New York, 1967) and A. Rabinowitch, *The Bolsheviks Come to Power* (New York, 1977).

It was not historians who initiated the dispute about the Bolshevik insurrection. The very men who eventually led the revolt first cast doubt on the wisdom of such a step. The controversial subject was broached for the first time by Lenin in two letters sent from Finland to the central committee of the Bolshevik party[2] in mid-September 1917: 'The Bolsheviks, having obtained a majority in the Soviets of Workers' and Soldiers' Deputies in both capitals, can and *must* take state power into their own hands.' According to Lenin 'armed insurrection' in Petrograd and Moscow was the only means which would lead to victory and this insurrection had to be treated 'as an art'.[3] A short note in the minutes of the central committee meeting of 15 September reveals the unease of those to whom Lenin addressed his demands. Stalin suggested that they should be reserved for further discussion by central organisations in the party; other comrades were anxious that suitable precautions be taken so that the letters would not become public knowledge; Kamenev proposed that Lenin's demands be rejected and he attempted to persuade the central committee to approve a resolution declaring 'all street action inadmissible at this time'. Finally the committee decided to take steps to 'prevent any actions in the barracks or the factories'.[4] This barely disguised rejection caused Lenin to tender his resignation from the central committee two weeks later, though he reserved his 'freedom to campaign among the *rank and file* of the party and at the Party Congress'.[5] Not until after Lenin's return to Petrograd did the central committee decide on 10 October (against the advice of Zinoviev and Kamenev) 'to place armed insurrection on the agenda'. It was decided that 'armed insurrection is unavoidable and imminent'.[6] However, this decision did not suspend opposition within the innermost circles of the party and the misunderstandings continued.

This review of the facts, which even Soviet historians do not

2. 'The Bolsheviks Must Assume Power. A Letter to the Central Committee and the Petrograd and Moscow Committees of the R.S.D.L.P. (B.)' (12–14 September 1917) in Lenin, *Collected Works* (Moscow, 1962), vol. 26, pp. 19–21; 'Marxism and Insurrection. A Letter to the Central Committee of the R.S.D.L.P. (b.)' (13–14 September 1917), ibid., pp. 22–7.

3. Ibid., pp. 26–7.

4. *Protokoly Tsentralnogo Komiteta RSDRP (B.) Avgust 1917–fevral' 1918* (Minutes of the Central Committee of the RSDLP. August 1917–February 1918) (Moscow, 1958), p. 55.

5. 'The Crisis Has Matured' (29 September 1917) in Lenin, *Collected Works*, vol. 26, p. 84.

6. *Protokoly Tsentral'nogo Komiteta RSDRP (b). Avgust 1917–fevral' 1918*, p. 178.

dispute, fails however get to the heart of the matter. Prior to October no one had anything but very vague, poorly conceived ideas about what was really meant by 'armed insurrection'. Those who spoke of an insurrection, whether to insist on it or to dismiss it, thought primarily in terms of the July Days in Petrograd, characterised by demonstrations in the streets by workers and soldiers, meetings with flags and banners, clashes with the police, unruly strikes and an uprising of the masses against the legally constituted authorities. This had been the outcome of agitation that was still not well organised and planned. The Bolshevik leadership did not trust in the elemental strength of the people and the attempted insurrection turned out to be a setback, not a prelude to political power. The uprising had the appearance of the classic insurrection typical of the revolutionary tradition in Europe ever since 1789. The battles on the barricades of 1848, the Paris Commune and the December Uprising in Moscow in 1905 were basically similar and yet, despite continual failure, this sort of insurrection had apparently lost none of its revolutionary appeal.

Even the Mensheviks did not turn their backs on the impending uprising in 1905.[7] In *Iskra*, their party newspaper, military experts discussed the best way to build barricades, the impact of artillery on street battles and the advantages and disadvantages of armed demonstrations by the masses. However, the meaning of 'insurrection' was never clearly defined and the party did not feel inclined to develop a definite plan or even to engage in conspiratorial activity. By 1905 the term 'general, popular insurrection' (*vseobshchee narodnoe vosstanie*) was in vogue all the way from the terrorist cells of the Socialist Revolutionaries to the liberal Kadets as a general description of the climax of the revolution. Such an uprising would require participation by the overwhelming majority of the people and would therefore represent a type of plebiscite. It would be a natural occurrence in a revolutionary process as unfathomable as nature itself. The legitimacy of such a popular event could never be doubted.

As long as tsarism was still intact, disagreements within the socialist camp centred on other matters. Disputes focused not on whether a mass uprising should be welcomed but on the proper role of the party in the revolution. This was the point at which the

This review of the facts, which even Soviet historians do not

7. For the discussion of 1905 see A. Fischer, *Russische Sozialdemokratie und bewaffneter Aufstand* (Wiesbaden, 1967).

disagreements between the Mensheviks and Bolsheviks widened
and eventually grew irreconcilable. The Mensheviks always claimed
that the Social Democratic Party could not possibly plan, organise
or 'make' the uprising which they foresaw. The masses themselves
would spawn the uprising and the party and its agitators would only
play a steering role. To think of planning or leading such an uprising
was considered to be adventurism, a conspiratorial phantasy and a
betrayal of the revolution. Lenin, to be sure, had always conceived
of the armed uprising as linked to mass popular disturbances
supported by broad strata of the population — peasants and proletarians alike. However, unlike his Menshevik opponents, Lenin
considered the insurrection to be at the heart of the party's strategy
for revolution. After 1901 Lenin demanded time and again that a
popular insurrection be prepared. By this he meant organising the
party in readiness for the moment of rebellion. This explains the
conspiratorial organisation of the Bolsheviks.[8] Professional revolutionaries should be prepared to take over the leadership of the
insurrection, to fight in the 'vanguard' of the rebellious masses, to
determine the political goals of the uprising and to aim and deliver
the final blow. If the party should fail when the people finally
proved capable of revolting, it would loose all reason to exist. When
the year 1905 arrived, Lenin's strategy was already fully developed.
After 'Bloody Sunday' in St Petersburg, the Bolshevik party congress in London was prepared to put it to the test.[9] However, the
revolutionary situation which Lenin anticipated did not materialise
on its own, as events soon demonstrated. Power and the victory of
'revolutionary democracy' were not won on the Presnya barricades
in December 1905.

When Lenin insisted in September 1917 that insurrection be
treated *as an art*, the political situation had changed dramatically.
Unchanged, however, was the role which insurrection still played in
Lenin's revolutionary strategy:

> To be successful, insurrection must rely not upon conspiracy and not
> upon a party, but upon the advanced class. This is the first point.
> Insurrection must rely upon a *revolutionary upsurge of the people*. This is
> the second point. Insurrection must rely upon that *turning-point in the
> history of the growing revolution* when the activity of the advanced ranks

8. Cf. D. Geyer, *Lenin in der russischen Sozialdemokratie* (Cologne, 1962), pp. 318–46.
9. *Tretii s-ezd RSDRP (b). Aprel'–Mai 1905. Protokoly*. (Third Congress of the RSDLP. April–May 1905. Minutes) (Moscow, 1959), pp. 98–160, 450–1.

of people is at its height, and when the *vacillations* in the ranks of the enemy and *in the ranks of the weak, half-hearted and irresolute friends of the revolution* are strongest. That is the third point. And these three conditions for raising the question of insurrection distinguish *Marxism from Blanquism*. Once these conditions exist, however, to refuse to treat insurrection as an *art* is a betrayal of Marxism and a betrayal of the revolution.

Dissension in the Bolshevik central committee did not revolve any longer around the question of whether this definition of insurrection could be reconciled with Marxist principles or whether the party would be guilty of 'Blanquism' if it adopted Lenin's views. Debate raged instead, firstly around Lenin's analysis of the revolutionary situation and secondly around the question of whether the party's political strategy should focus on insurrection. Lenin's theses insisted that now, in September 1917, all the 'objective conditions for the victory of the insurrection' clearly existed: the support of the class that formed the 'vanguard of the revolution'; a 'country–wide revolutionary upsurge' of the people; 'vacillation on a serious political scale among our enemies and among the irresolute petty bourgeoisie' and a turning–point in the history of the revolution which henceforth lent it a 'popular character'.[11] There were of course no iron-clad guarantees that these assertions were correct.

Lenin had even forged further ahead: 'It would be naïve', he said, 'to wait for a "formal" majority for the Bolsheviks. No revolution ever waits for that.' Lenin had an original view, unrelated to votes or elections, of what constituted a majority. From the fact that the Bolsheviks controlled the majority in the Petrograd and Moscow soviets, Lenin concluded: 'We have the following of the majority of a *class*, the vanguard of the revolution, the vanguard of the people.' After the Kornilov revolt the Mensheviks and Socialist Revolutionaries had refused a coalition with the Kadets. This meant to Lenin that they had 'clearly lost their majority among the people'. Since Agriculture Minister Chernov proved incapable of resolving the agrarian question Lenin concluded: 'We have the following of the majority of the people. . . . *Our* victory is assured for the people are close to desperation, and we are showing the entire people a sure way out.'[12] One can understand why Lenin's comrades did not

10. 'Marxism and Insurrection', *Collected Works*, vol. 26, p. 22f.
11. Ibid., p. 23.
12. Ibid., p. 24.

immediately grasp his logic (a majority in the Petrograd and Moscow soviets = a majority among the vanguard of the people = a majority among the people = victory for the Bolsheviks in the revolution). The reliability of Lenin's assurances remained in doubt. At the very moment of armed insurrection, leading figures in the party were still not fully confident that it would succeed.

In September 1917, while Lenin claimed that 'the moment is ripe for insurrection' the *political* consequences of his theories still encountered strong resistance. For the first time since the fiasco of the July Days, the party felt rehabilitated in the eyes of 'revolutionary democracy'. Party membership had multiplied as a result of the struggle against the Kornilov revolt and the Bolshevik programme of immediate action to give the masses land and peace was winning support in the army and among the workers. The Bolshevik majority in the Petrograd and Moscow soviets and the catastrophic losses suffered by the Mensheviks in the municipal elections were sure signs of Bolshevik strength. With Lenin's approval, in September the party once again took up the slogan 'all power to the soviets'. This was the cry which the Bolsheviks wished to advance at the 'Democratic Conference' called at Kerensky's initiative for 18 September. The chances for success in radicalising soviet democracy did indeed seem fairly good at the time. There was reason to hope, thanks to the pressure of the masses, that the Provisional Government would soon be replaced with a soviet government — a coalition in which the Bolsheviks would play a key role. Bolshevik declarations at the Conference were in keeping with such prospects: 'Our party has never and does not now try to seize power against the will of the organised majority of the working masses.'[14] In comparison with progressing towards power through soviet democracy, Lenin's course must have seemed risky and even adventurist.

One should note, however, that Lenin never repudiated the alternatives to civil war in the articles he wrote during September for the party newspaper *Rabochii Put'*. If power was transferred to the soviets, Lenin did not exclude the possibility of a 'peaceful evolution of the revolution', compromises with the Mensheviks and Socialist Revolutionaries and a non-Bolshevik soviet government

13. *Protokoly Tsentral'nogo Komiteta RSDRP (b). Avgust 1917–fevral' 1918* (Moscow, 1958), pp. 93–104.
14. 'Deklaratsiya fraktsii bol'shevikov, oglashennaya na Vserossiiskom Demokraticheskom Soveshchanii' (Declaration of the Bolshevik faction at the Democratic Conference) (18 September 1917), ibid., p. 51.

with the Bolsheviks in opposition. In an article which appeared on 16 September Lenin stated that 'only an alliance of the Bolsheviks with the Socialist-Revolutionaries and Mensheviks, only an immediate transfer of all power to the Soviets would make civil war in Russia impossible'.[15] Indeed, on 27 September, two days before Lenin offered his resignation, the party paper noted:

> By seizing full power, the Soviets could still today — and this is probably their last chance — ensure the peaceful development of the revolution, peaceful elections of deputies by the people, and a peaceful struggle of parties inside the Soviets.... Power could pass peacefully from one party to another.[16]

What was implied here was only in apparent contradiction to Lenin's insistence that the party should prepare for insurrection. The alternative between civil war and 'the peaceful path' of revolution only existed if the Provisional Government had previously collapsed and all power had devolved on the soviets. Armed insurrection remained the means to bring this about. Lenin therefore proposed soviet democracy primarily for agitational purposes as part of the struggle for power. He was concerned not least with gaining the support of a party whose leading figures were concentrating on legal political work instead of on an uprising. On 21 September the central committee acceded to the majority vote of the Bolshevik faction in the Democratic Conference and agreed to participate in the 'pre-parliament' convoked by Kerensky.[17] Lenin bitterly denounced this 'peaceful', parliamentary path and there is no doubt that he was no longer willing to compromise.

One can, therefore, say that Lenin's position after September 1917 rested on three dialectically linked axioms:

(1) Anyone who supported the Bolshevik slogan, 'all power to the soviets', must break with those parties that had been the main support of 'revolutionary democracy';

(2) Anyone who desired soviet government of this kind must decide in favour of an insurrection;

(3) Anyone who decided in favour of an insurrection was voting for a Bolshevik soviet.

15. 'The Russian Revolution and the Civil War' (16 September 1917) in Lenin, *Collected Works*, vol. 26, p. 36.
16. 'The Tasks of the Revolution' (26/27 September 1917), ibid., p. 67f.
17. *Protokoly Tsentral'nogo Komiteta RSDRP (b). Avgust–fevral' 1918* (Moscow, 1958), p. 65.

In his first letters on insurrection Lenin had already urged that the Democratic Conference should be confronted with a forceful ultimatum insisting on complete acceptance of the Bolshevik programme. Without waiting for an answer, the Bolsheviks should then leave the Conference and immediately return to the masses in the factories and barracks:

> Their place is there, the pulse of life is there, there is the source of salvation for our revolution. . . . There in ardent and impassioned speeches, we must explain our programme and put the alternative: either the Conference adopts it *in its entirety*, or else insurrection. There is no middle course. Delay is impossible. The revolution is dying. By putting the question in this way . . . *we shall be able to determine the right moment to start the insurrection.*[18]

The passion with which Lenin attempted to stir the party into action is abundantly clear from the letters he wrote to the central committee and in the vigorous appeals he made to party organisations and conferences. Increasingly vehement, he boycotted the pre-parliament and condemned the 'absolute idiocy' and 'complete betrayal' of those who wanted to wait until the All-Russian Congress of Soviets. In passionate argument he insisted again and again that insurrection was an art, a problem of technique and organisation. As an introduction Lenin drew on the experiences which Engels describes in his pamphlet 'Revolution and Counter-Revolution in Germany'. Lenin never tired of presenting these abbreviated remarks on insurrection as the great legacy of Danton and Marx which the party was compelled to respect.[19]

One cannot fail to be impressed by the strength of Lenin's conviction that there was no time to lose; if power was to be seized and consolidated, action had to be taken — it was a case of now or never: 'It is my profound conviction that if we "wait" for the Congress of Soviets and let the present moment pass, we shall *ruin* the *revolution.*'[20] So far as Lenin was concerned, victory was assured. His analysis of the social and military situation convinced him that the insurrection would succeed. One could strike simultaneously in three different localities: Moscow, Petrograd and Finland. Moreover, this time the army would not advance on the

18. Lenin, *Collected Works*, vol. 26, p. 27.
19. 'Advice of an Onlooker' (8 October 1917), *ibid.*, p. 179; Lenin thought this pamphlet was a work of Karl Marx.
20. 'The Crisis Has Matured', ibid., p. 84.

insurgents. Government disarray, the disintegration of the Mensheviks and Socialist Revolutionaries and agitation for land and peace would secure the Bolsheviks majority support in the country.[21] All these claims should not be considered individually. Lenin's arguments were inspired by the battle he was forced to wage within his own party and polemic infused his analysis of reality. This is the reason for the exaggeration in his political views. Lenin took rural unrest and transformed it into a mighty peasant revolt which would soon erupt. Consequently, the Bolsheviks would be 'miserable traitors' to the peasants, democracy and freedom if they did not take action to assist the uprising.[22] Lenin continually pointed to signs of crisis within the belligerent nations of Europe so that the insurrection would appear to be part of an international revolution. Reports of mass arrests of Italian comrades and of incipient mutinies in the German fleet were stylised by Lenin into 'indisputable symptoms that a great turning-point is at hand, that we are *on the eve of a world-wide revolution'.* Here the old idea once more emerged that the Bolsheviks were destined to serve as the vanguard of the international proletariat. By means of insurrection they would 'save, the world revolution . . . the Russian Revolution . . . and the lives of hundreds of thousands of people at the front'.[23]

We cannot say for sure why Lenin was so utterly convinced, how he could have gained such complete confidence in his theses. Possible answers cannot exclude the psychology of the man, but psychology does not excuse us from searching for rational explanations. We know for certain that Lenin considered the military difficulties of the uprising to be intimately related to the political problems. On 24 September Lenin wrote that 'history has made the *military* question now the fundamental *political* question.[24] He may have culled the underlying insight from Clausewitz: 'Armed uprising is a *special* form of political struggle', is therefore politics 'with other means'. A quotation from Marx completed Lenin's argument: 'Insurrection is an art quite as much as war'.[25] Each passing moment and every military or technical calculation had a

21. Ibid.
22. Ibid., p. 81.
23. 'Letter to the Central Committee, the Moscow and Petrograd Committees and the Bolshevik Members of the Petrograd and Moscow Soviets' (1 October 1917), ibid., p. 140.
24. 'Letter to the Chairman of the Regional Committee of the Army, Navy and Workers of Finland' (27 September 1917), ibid., p. 69.
25. 'Advice of an Onlooker', ibid., p. 179f. Cf. Hahlweg, 'Lenin and Clausewitz', *Arkhiv für Kulturgeschichte* 36 (1954), pp. 30–59, 357–87.

place in the political strategy of revolution. Lenin's thesis that every delay was a crime could therefore be detached from a given day and hour and reiterated along with new arguments arising from the changing conditions: there was a danger of a separate peace between the imperialists; Kerensky wanted to deliver revolutionary Petrograd to the Germans; a second Kornilov revolt was imminent; 'the success of both the Russian and world revolutions depends on two or three days' fighting'.[26]

By 10 October Lenin had succeeded in finding a majority in the Bolshevik central committee for his policy of insurrection. An important step in this direction was taken when the Bolshevik faction decided to walk out of the opening meeting of the Pre-Parliament on 7 October. On the same day, Lenin arrived from Finland and took up quarters on Vasilevskii Island in Petrograd. Three days later the central committee voted in favour of his thesis that the time was ripe for an insurrection. This decision was probably justified by the worsening situation in Petrograd, where the government was clearly heading for another serious crisis.[27] By October its authority was crumbling. The military situation on the northern front was catastrophic. The loyalty of the large garrison in the capital was in doubt. Shortages of food and fuel continued and prices rose accordingly. There was every reason to fear the worst. In the suburbs and factories the listlessness of workers looked likely to galvanise into riot and rebellion. All the passion the Council of the Republic could muster did not compensate for the widespread misery. Prominent Mensheviks and Socialist Revolutionaries sat on the executive committee of the All-Russian Soviet but they were no less isolated than the government. The Congress of Soviets, due to convene on 20 October, was likely to reinforce Bolshevik ascendancy. Left-wing SRs supported the Bolsheviks and the Petrograd Soviet was dominated by Trotsky, the chief spokesman of the Bolshevik majority. When the Congress of Soviets of the Northern Region met in the Smolnyi Institute on 11 October, hostility to the government erupted in demonstrations which approached a formal declaration of war. Lenin had high hopes that this Congress would become insurrectionary and that the Baltic Fleet and Finnish troops

26. Lenin, *Collected Works*, vol. 26, p. 181.
27. Cf. the informative study based on archival material of Z.V. Stepanov, *Rabochie Petrograda v period podgotovki i provedeniya Oktyabr'skogo vooruzhennogo vosstaniya* (Petrograd workers during the preparation and execution of the armed October uprising) (Moscow–Leningrad, 1965).

could be persuaded to march on Petrograd. The central committee's decision to prepare an insurrection seemed to have come at just the right moment.[28]

On closer examination, however, it is clear that the Bolshevik leadership was still avoiding a final decision on 10 October. Plans for an insurrection and the seizure of power were not discussed. Instead, protests from Kamenev and Zinoviev led to a further rehashing of old controversies. An insurrection, they asserted, would drive the petty bourgeoisie into the arms of the Kadets and result in defeat. A proletarian government would be incapable of pursuing the revolutionary war against German imperialism and most soldiers would abandon the Bolsheviks. Lenin's thesis that most of the Russian people and the world proletariat already supported the Bolsheviks was simply not true. The party's chances of success lay therefore not in an uprising but in defensive action, in exploiting the forthcoming All-Russian Congress of Soviets and in concentrating on elections to the Constituent Assembly.[29] Lenin was once more compelled to take up the exhausting struggle to win approval for his strategy of insurrection.[30] The arguments advanced by his opponents had some historical justification but little practical relevance; they were finding it difficult to keep abreast of the rapidly changing situation.

In the end, this dispute was of little consequence. Appeals for an insurrection became unnecessary when another means was found to topple the government. (It seems likely that Trotsky, the chairman of the Petrograd Soviet, played a large part in developing this phase of Bolshevik strategy.) On 6 October rumours about a counter-revolutionary plot began to circulate among the soldiers.[31] The government was allegedly preparing to abandon Petrograd, the citadel of revolution, to the advancing Germans. In a momentous decision, Trotsky resolved to do all he could to exploit this rumour. In the declaration which he wrote as part of the Bolshevik boycott of the pre-parliament, Trotsky conjured up a 'mortal danger' which was

28. 'Letter to the Bolshevik Comrades Attending the Congress of Soviets of the Northern Region' (8 October 1917), *Collected Works*, vol. 26, pp. 182–7.

29. G. Zinov'ev and Yu. Kamenev, 'K tekushchemu momentu' (On the Present Situation) (11 October 1917) in *Protokoly Tsentral'nogo Komiteta RSDRP (b). Avgust 1917–fevral' 1918* (Moscow, 1958), pp. 87–92.

30. Cf. Lenin, 'Letter to the Comrades' (17 October), 'Letter to the Bolshevik Party Members' (19 October 1917), *Collected Works*, vol. 26, pp. 195–227.

31. 'Rezolyutsiya Soldatskoi Sektsii Petrogradskogo Soveta' (Resolution of the soldiers' section of the Petrograd Soviet) (6 October 1917), cf. L. Trotskii, *Sochineniya (Works)*, vol. III, 1, p. 321.

menacing the capital: Kerensky was planning to move the government to Moscow in order to create a bulwark of counter-revolution and destroy the Constituent Assembly. The garrison would allegedly be evacuated soon, Petrograd would be sacrificed to the German army and the revolution would be stamped out.[32] Trotsky evidently recognised the potential of this thesis. If the Bolsheviks succeeded in making the rumour seem credible, a powerful reaction would bolster the efforts of the Petrograd Soviet to organise a broad front of resistance. Trotsky understood the kind of appeal which needed to be sent out to the garrison and the workers — not a call for insurrection but a call for defence of the Russian capital against internal and external enemies, against counter-revolution in the shape of Milyukov and Kaiser Wilhelm. The Petrograd Bolsheviks thus hit upon a formula with strong appeal to the instincts of the masses. Party agitation became concentrated and focused on a concrete goal: breaking the hold of the officer corps over the garrison and transferring command of the troops to the Petrograd Soviet. In addition, the Bolsheviks attempted to prime the workers to arm themselves and support the rebellion of the garrison.

The Petrograd Soviet quickly realised what a golden opportunity had fallen to it. Regiments were urged to go on the alert as early as 9 October.[33] Two days later, Trotsky took advantage of speeches he was to deliver before the Congress of the Northern Region to spread far and wide his appeal for the defence of the capital.[34] Troops well outside Petrograd, especially in the Baltic Fleet and on the northern front, had to be integrated with the plan to seize power.[35] The Bolshevik strategy benefitted greatly from the legal status of the soviets and preparations for the insurrection were open and well disciplined. On 15 October Russians could even read in their Sunday newspapers that the Bolsheviks were plotting a coup.[36]

32. 'Deklaratsiya fraktsii bol'shevikov na zasedanii Demokraticheskogo Soveshchaniya' (Declaration of the Bolshevik faction at a session of the Democratic Conference) (7 October 1917), ibid., pp. 321–3; cf. also *Protokoly Tsentral'nogo Komiteta*, pp. 77–9.
33. 'Rezolyutsiya Petrogradskogo Soveta o vyvode voisk iz Petrograda' (Resolution of the Petrograd Soviet on the withdrawal of troops from Petrograd) (9 October 1917), L. Trotskii, *Sochineniya*, vol. III, 1, p. 327.
34. Ibid., pp. 5–14.
35. On the role of the Baltic fleet in October 1917 see *Baltiiskie moryaki v podgotovke i provedenii Velikoi Oktyabr'skoi revolyutsii* (Baltic sailors and the preparation and execution of the Great October Revolution) Moscow–Leningrad, 1957); *Protokoly i postanovleniya Tsentral'nogo Komiteta Baltiiskogo flota, 1917–1918* (Minutes and decisions of the central committee of the Baltic fleet, 1917–18) (Moscow–Leningrad, 1963).
36. *Delo Naroda*, no. 181 (15 October 1917) in Browder and Kerensky, *The*

The following day, Trotsky declared before a plenary session of the Soviet: 'It is said that we are preparing a group to seize power. We make no secret of this. . . .'[37] The Military Revolutionary Committee (MRC), formed on 11 October as the centre of operations, was not a cabal but a duly elected institution of the Petrograd Soviet.[38] This meant that it had access to many channels of communication: it had its own newspapers and enjoyed regular contact with army regiments and district soviets within the city,[39] trade unions, factory committees, the workers' militia and the Red Guards.[40] While the government stood by helplessly, the MRC surrounded it and systematically whittled away at its power.

The wisdom of these tactics is evidenced by the fact that even the Bolshevik central committee could now be persuaded to turn its attention to practical matters. On 16 October it decided in favour of permanent representation on the MRC.[41] A rash of concerns arose and were again discussed at length. When the debate turned to insurrection many comrades were still mesmerised by the July fiasco. Furthermore, the reports of local party representatives on the chances for victory were not clearly affirmative. In the end, the view prevailed that power could be seized only if the garrison resisted the government and was willing to take defensive action against measures which directly threatened the troops. This analysis seemed to conform with the views of the Petrograd Soviet. Trotsky's strategy thus triumphed, even though no tangible successes had yet been achieved. It was agreed that in order to seize power the garrison would have to be commandeered and the MRC would

Provisional Government, vol. III, pp. 1764f.; cf. F. Dan's allusion to Bolshevik plans for an uprising (14 October), *Izvestiya CIK*, no. 198 (15 October 1917) in *Velikaya Oktyabr'skaya Sotsialisticheskaya Revolyutsiya. Khronika sobytii IV* (Moscow, 1961), p. 429.

37. L. Trotskii, *Sochineniya*, vol. III, 2, p. 15.

38. Important material can be found in *Petrogradksii Voenno-Revolyutsionnyi Komitet: Dokumenty i materialy*, vols. I–III (Moscow, 1966/67); cf. *Velikaya Oktyabr'skaya Sotsialisticheskaya revolyutsiya. Dokumenty i materialy: Oktyabr'skoe vooruzhennoe vosstanie v Petrograde* (The Great Socialist October Revolution. Documents and Materials. The armed October insurrection in Petrograd) (Moscow, 1957).

39. See *Raionnye Sovety Petrograda v 1917 godu. Protokoly, rezolyutsii, postanovleniya obshchikh sobranii i zasedanii ispolnitel'nykh komitetov*, vols. I–III (The Petrograd raion soviets in 1917) (Moscow–Leningrad, 1964–6).

40. V.I. Startsev, 'Voenno-revolyutsionnyi Komitet i Krasnaya gvardiya v Oktyabr'skom vooruzhennom vosstanii' (The Military Revolutionary Committee and the Red Guard in the armed October insurrection) in *Oktyabr'skoe vooruzhennoe vosstanie v Petrograde: Sbornik statei* (Moscow–Leningrad, 1957), pp. 106–41.

41. *Protokoly Tsentral'nogo Komiteta RSDRP (b). Avgust 1917–fevral' 1918* (Moscow, 1958), p. 104.

slowly have to supplant the Petrograd officer corps. The task for the next few days was to provoke the government and thus to initiate the transfer of power.

These tactics were so unlike the familiar understanding of the insurrection that Trotsky was able to exploit the resulting confusion in order to cloak further preparations. The government, the bourgeois press and even the Mensheviks expected that Bolshevik agitation would lead once again as in July to armed demonstrations by the masses. Thus, Maxim Gorky on 18 October: 'An unorganised mob will rush into the streets ... and adventurers, thieves and professional murderers ... will begin to write the History of the Russian Revolution'.[42] Trotsky answered on the same day that nothing had been decided which was not already public knowledge. If the Soviet — 'this revolutionary parliament — deems it necessary to call for demonstrations, then it will do so. ... We have still not set a date for the attack'.[43] All measures taken by the MRC, including arming the workers' militia, were still portrayed as purely defensive. The bourgeoisie, not the Soviet, was allegedly seeking conflict; it was the counter-revolution which was 'mobilising all its forces against the workers and peasants'. Trotsky announced that any attempt to subvert the approaching All-Russian Congress of Soviets or to deprive Petrograd of its garrison would be answered 'with a steadfast counter-offensive that will be pursued to the finish'.[44] Such declarations seemed to imply that the struggle would only be unleashed if initiated by the government.

Bolshevik agitation now focused on the suspicion that the Congress of Soviets was in danger. Trotsky could not forgo the Congress if his plan of slowly easing into power was to succeed. At all costs, he said, the deputies must be free to fulfil their appointed role, namely: 'to approve resolutions on the transfer of power to the All-Russian Congress of Soviets, the immediate conclusion of a cease-fire on all fronts and the conveyance of all land to the peasants.'[45] Until the Congress met, the means had to be safeguarded of employing the legal authority of the Petrograd Soviet to authorise the organisation of a *coup d'état*. This meant that the Bolsheviks could not transgress the rules of the Soviet. Victory

42. *Novaya Zhizn'* no. 156 (18 October 1917) in Browder and Kerensky, *The Provisional Government*, vol. III, p. 1766.
43. L. Trotskii, *Sochineniya*, vol. III, 2, pp. 31–3. A second version of Trotsky's speech is in Browder and Kerensky, p. 1767.
44. Ibid.
45. Ibid.

would be achieved not by pressuring the comrades to initiate an insurrection but by continually widening the authority of the Soviet. So far as Trotsky was concerned, treating 'insurrection as an art' meant treating the legality of the Soviet as an art. Even some members of the MRC probably believed that they were working, not towards an insurrection, but simply to protect the Congress and the garrison against counter-revolutionary violence. As late as 24 October discussions based on this assumption were held with the Socialist Revolutionaries.[46]

We know that even Lenin failed to fathom the logic of this approach and to comprehend Trotsky's strategy. Tying the seizure of power to decisions taken by the Congress struck him as totally unacceptable: 'It is death to wait.' The Congress was of interest to Lenin only if it met after the insurrection had occurred and if the deputies were confined to rubber-stamping the Bolshevik victory. In a state of extreme agitation, he wrote on the evening of 24 October just before taking the tram to the Smolnyi Institute:

> With all my might I urge comrades to realise that everything now hangs by a thread; that we are confronted by problems which are not to be solved by conferences or congresses. . . . but exclusively by peoples, by the masses, by the struggle of the armed people.

Furthermore, he demanded categorically that 'the matter be decided without fail this very evening, or this very night'.[47] In fact, not much remained to be done. The Provisional Government was but an empty shell, already powerless for all practical purposes. It relied for security on a few hundred rifles and the vain hope that military relief was on the way. Already on 21 October the Petrograd Soviet had set the changeover of power in motion. According to the plans, the first step was an ultimatum addressed to the government's military staff under Colonel Polkovnikov. The Soviet demanded that he recognise the commissars whom it named and that all military orders be approved by the MRC.[48] This amounted to a demand for capitulation. The seizure of power began on 23 October when the Soviet claimed sole authority over the Petrograd garrison. Most regiments submitted to the Smolnyi and the cossacks main-

46. *Golos soldata* (25 October 1917) in *Petrogradskii Voenno-Revolyutsionnyi Komitet*, vol. I, p. 99.
47. Lenin, *Collected Works*, vol. 26, p. 234f.
48. *Petrogradksii Voenno-Revolyutsionnyi Komitet*, vol. I, p. 59.

tained their neutrality; a call went out to the Petrograd citizenry to remain calm and composed.[49]

What happened next resembled a security operation. No insurrection was proclaimed; the 'armed masses' were not summoned onto the streets and their military strength was not put to the test. The government itself gave the final signal in the early morning of 24 October when it attempted to shut down the Bolshevik press. The rest seems almost trivial. A macabre scene occurred in the Mariinsky Palace when Kerensky actually had to inform the Council of the Republic that the Russian capital was in revolt.[50] The next day, the victors proclaimed their triumph even before sailors from Kronstadt could land and the cruiser *Aurora* could prepare to open fire: 'The Provisional Government has fallen. The government has passed into the hands. . . . of the Military Revolutionary Committee which stands at the head of the Petrograd proletariat and garrison.'[51] The isolated military skirmishes which still flared up on 25 October were due to the cabinet decision to remain in session in the Malachite Room of the Winter Palace, despite the absence of the Prime Minister.

Kerensky's fall was a brilliant success for Trotsky and his strategy for seizing power. However, the ease with which power was achieved points to other factors as well. The Petrograd garrison which submitted to Bolshevik orders was not strong enough to withstand a serious military challenge. The effectiveness of the workers' militia and the Red Guards is also in doubt. Hence, the Petrograd coup was not due primarily to the military power which the MRC was able to deploy. It was instead the fruit of the *political* victory which the Bolsheviks had won earlier under the soviet democracy — a system whose principles they repudiated even though it was indispensible to them.[52] The *coup d'état* could not have been organised if the Petrograd Soviet had not been under firm control: the government could only be disarmed physically because it had already been disarmed politically. By the same token, the government could not make use of its power because it was not backed up with political

49. Ibid., pp. 67, 97f.
50. *Rech'* no. 251 (25 October 1917); cf. Browder and Kerensky, *The Provisional Government*, vol. III, pp. 1172–4.
51. 'K grazhdanam Rossii' (To the citizens of Russia) in *Petrogradskii Voenno-Revolyutsionnyi Komitet*, vol. I, p. 106.
52. Anweiler, *Die Rätebewegung in Rußland, 1905–1921* (Leiden, 1958), pp. 180–241. For the seizure of power in the provinces see J.L.H. Keep, *The Russian Revolution. A Study in Mass Mobilization* (New York, 1976).

strength. The art of insurrection flowed from political skills and policies whose plebiscitary nature can hardly be contested. Even the Mensheviks and Socialist Revolutionaries attempted at the last moment to take a leaf from the Bolshevik book in order to escape being caught between the Scylla of counter-revolution and the Charybdis of Bolshevik dictatorship. However, when faced with Bolshevik proposals for an immediate truce and the redistribution of the land, no other alternative was politically viable by October. This was the overriding factor. It led to the fall not just of the Provisional Government but of soviet democracy as well.

9

Democracy and Revolution

Among the political consequences of the October Revolution must be counted the demise of parliamentary democracy — even before it could begin to develop its institutions. What had appeared to be the natural development of the February Revolution withered away and the experiment in democracy, for which the Constituent Assembly was supposed to lay firm foundations, was supplanted by Bolshevik rule. The victors promised to institute the dictatorship of the proletariat within a newly founded Soviet Socialist Republic. The question has often been raised of whether this failure of democracy was inevitable or at least a logical outcome. In other words, does the Bolshevik victory prove that Russia was still unable, because of its social and political backwardness, to generate the democratic, Western-style constitution which had been expected in 1917?[1]

Convincing answers are not easy to find. The evidence which can be offered is vitiated by the extreme conditions which prevailed: Russia was in the midst of a war and the political structure, indeed the whole society, was in turmoil. Everything we know of the pre-history of the Revolution indicates that 'bourgeois' democracy had only limited prospects for success. The bourgeois parties were supported by only a tiny fraction of the population. Even under more normal conditions, like those existing immediately after the collapse of the old regime, a democratic, parliamentary constitution would not necessarily have prospered. After the events of February, revolution and near anarchy swept the country. The narrow social strata whose political convictions most closely approximated 'democracy' as understood in the West had hoped for as quiet and painless a cabinet reshuffle as possible in order to effect the transfer

---

1. See the discussion in D.S. Anin, 'The February Revolution: Was the Collapse Inevitable?', *Soviet Studies* XVIII, no. 4 (1967), pp. 435–57. For the Soviet dispute with Western researchers see the article by G.Z. Ioffe in *Istoricheskie zapiski* 78 (1965), pp. 3–30.

of power to the Duma. After the collapse of the monarchy, however, large sections of the population began to intervene in political affairs and they compelled these narrow strata to explore beyond their own political programme.[2] Revolution as a mass event overturned many political plans. Not only was the Autocracy destroyed but even hopes for a constitutional monarchy, the intermediate form of government under which Russian liberals hoped to nurture political freedom. The politically informed sector of tsarist society was forced to embrace democratic policies whose underlying concepts and standards were not its own. Because of its narrow social base, this sector was unable to assimilate the huge, liberated populations and to channel their political energies into institutions which did not yet even exist. The Revolution was necessary to spark the development of democratic, parliamentary institutions; once unleashed, however, it possessed an inner dynamic which could not be controlled. This dilemma was in evidence from the outset in the confrontation between the soviets and the Provisional Government.

These pessimistic conclusions about the prospects for parliamentary democracy in Russia are not beyond dispute. One could point out that both the Socialist Revolutionaries and the Menshevik Social Democrats — powerful groups within the soviets — favoured democracy and a parliamentary republic. After the February Revolution, republicanism became the sole hope of the liberals and was also supported by most politically organised socialists during the spring and summer of 1917. The government and the majority in the soviets (i.e. liberals and socialists alike) believed that the great decisions about the revolution should not be taken in the streets but should be held in abeyance until the All-Russian Constituent Assembly could meet. In fact, the demand for a Constituent Assembly was so general that there was good reason to believe that it would indeed lay firm foundations for Russian democracy despite all the divisions in society. However, one must not overlook the fact that the various parties had very different motives for urging a Constituent Assembly. The apparent democratic consensus was not very profound. The Provisional Government (in all its changing phases and compositions) found its own legitimacy reinforced by the fact that a Constituent Assembly was to be convened. It therefore had no reason to rush. As long as no elected parliament yet existed, the

2. Trotsky quite rightly emphasised this feature when he said that the undeniable hallmark of the Revolution was the direct participation by the masses in historical events (*The History of the Russian Revolution*).

government could justify its inaction by claiming that all vital questions had to be postponed until they could be finally resolved by the supreme authority, the Constituent Assembly.[3]

This excuse covered more than mere indecision. A programme of sweeping reform could not possibly have been undertaken while the war was still in progress. As long as continuation of the war remained the highest priority of the government, it had no desire to convoke the Constituent Assembly. This probably explains why elections were repeatedly postponed. No emergency government wishes to be replaced by a democratic parliament. Kerensky in particular had good reason to resist submitting the supreme authority which he had acquired to the test of a parliamentary vote. If Russia was to remain within the Alliance, the Prime Minister needed the acclamation of the public, not interference from parliament. If he was to alleviate the worsening crisis and restore stability, he required a sympathetic hearing at pseudo-parliamentary events, not a democratically elected national assembly. Kerensky thus hoped to recover the support he had lost in the soviets. He employed this technique time and again between August and October: at the Moscow State Conference and the Democratic Conference, in the so-called pre-parliament and the Council of the Republic. This ploy also lay behind the formal dissolution of the old imperial Duma on 1 September and the ensuing proclamation of the Russian Republic.[4] (The Committee of the imperial Duma had clung to the legal claim that it constituted the highest authority in the land until the Constituent Assembly met.) Kerensky's strategy was to take only intermediate steps and always to postpone the final decision. Most Socialist Revolutionaries and Mensheviks acquiesced in this strategy. The war required delay.

Those who argue that postponing the elections was a fateful mistake, largely responsible for the failure of the democratic experiment in Russia, usually overlook the parlous political situation in which the government found itself. If the Constituent Assembly had met, it would have been compelled to tackle without delay a number of extremely thorny issues. Solutions were needed to such pressing problems as the constitutional place of the soviets in the new state and, above all, the great land reform and the restructuring

---

3. Documents and contemporary comments on the Constituent Assembly can be found in Browder and Kerensky, *The Provisional Government*, vol. I, pp. 434ff.

4. The deliberations of the Moscow State Conference were published by Ya.A. Yakovlev: *Gosudarstvennoe soveshchanie* (Tsentrarkhiv. 1917g. v dokumentakh i materialakh) (Moscow–Leningrad, 1930).

of the Russian Empire into a federal, multinational state. Decisions such as these were likely to provoke serious consequences and probably would have scuttled further participation in a military alliance which Russia was already barely able to maintain. The price of reform was likely to be a separate peace with the Central Powers and the evacuation of vast stretches of the Empire, including Poland. With the notable exception of the Bolsheviks, no one was willing to bear such a responsibility. When Kerensky was finally deposed, the provisional date for the much postponed elections was 12 (25) November 1917. As everybody knows, the Bolsheviks intervened and seized power.

The government's *attentisme* was as dangerous as it was comprehensible. Bolshevik agitators enjoyed great success in using the delay in order to accuse official policy-makers of purposely deceiving the people and flouting their will. So arose the paradoxical situation that the very party which rejected parliamentarism in principle as a reactionary form of government could heap blame on republicans who hesitated to place Russia in the hands of a democratic parliament only as long as the crisis and the war continued.

After the Bolsheviks had seized power and the Provisional Government had collapsed, Lenin no longer wished to convene a Constituent Assembly for obvious reasons. However, denouncing the future parliament would have proven very unpopular at that time. Lenin therefore felt obliged to declare publicly the day after the seizure of power that the new regime was simply a provisional government — the same formula used by the government which had just been overthrown. The Council of People's Commissars was a 'Provisional Government of Workers and Peasants' which would take over the government only 'until the Constituent Assembly is convened'. This Assembly reserved all rights to make final determinations about the decrees of the new government.[5] Lenin of course never intended to honour these assurances. However, the fact that the revolutionaries felt compelled to employ such tactics indicates that considerable sympathy for democratic parliamentarism was still thought to exist among broad strata of the population. Like the preceding governments, the Bolsheviks wished to avoid any measures that might have undermined their still unconsolidated power. Further evidence of this concern can be found in the

5. Resolution on the creation of the Council of People's Commissars on 26 October 1917.

decision of the Bolshevik central committee not to postpone again the election date set by Kerensky.

Thus free elections to a Constituent Assembly were held in Bolshevik Russia three weeks after Red October. They were the first (and last) universal, equal, direct and secret elections that Russia has ever seen. There is no doubt that those who permitted them found the whole situation deeply distasteful. On 17 (30) November *Pravda* was already proclaiming that the Constituent Assembly had but one duty: to proclaim the Republic of Workers', Soldiers' and Peasants' Deputies and then dissolve itself. In the course of the propaganda barrage which ensued, Lenin announced 'the strongest, fastest, most decisive and energetic measures' if the Assembly failed to recognise unreservedly 'the soviet government, the soviet revolution'.[6] The announcement of the election results only increased the Bolsheviks' disgust. The reason becomes apparent if one looks at the figures.

The results seemed to indicate that at this time the people favoured a parliamentary republic or at least were opposed to dictatorship by the Bolsheviks. If districts in the Ukraine are included, more than half of all electors, or upwards of twenty million people, gave their vote to the Socialist Revolutionaries. Only about 1.3 million voted for the Menshevik list and almost two million supported the Kadets.[7] The Bolsheviks, who had increased their strength enormously, drew almost ten million votes. However, the distribution of seats revealed that a government drawn from the centre of the Constituent Assembly would have formed a solid majority faced with strong parliamentary opposition from the Bolsheviks. Three hundred and seventy Socialist Revolutionaries, allied with the small Menshevik and Kadet groupings and supported by the non-Russian deputies, could probably have rallied an impressive majority of 480 deputies as opposed to 175 Bolshevik deputies and their left SR sympathisers. Lenin reacted on 6 (19) January 1918 by sending a detachment of sailors to the Tauride Palace to disperse the Constituent Assembly.[8] Does this demons-

6. O. Anweiler, *Die Rätebewegung in Rußland, 1905–1921* (Leiden, 1958), pp. 267ff. See also A. Kropat, 'Lenin und die Konstituierende Versammlung in Rußland', *Jahrbücher für die Geschichte Osteuropas* 5 (1957), pp. 488–98. See the documents in J. Bunyan and H.H. Fisher, *The Bolshevik Revolution 1917–1918. Documents and Materials* (Stanford, repr. 1961), pp. 338ff.

7. For the conduct of the elections and for their outcome see the analysis of O.H. Radkey, *The Elections to the Russian Constituent Assembly of 1917* (Cambridge, Mass., 1950).

8. For the meetings and the discussions which took place see the minutes *Vseros-*

trate, as was claimed subsequently, that Lenin was prepared to ride roughshod over the will of the people?

The Bolsheviks answered this question of course with a resounding no. The Assembly, they claimed, did not reflect the true intentions of the masses: the electoral results were based on lists which had been drawn up before the October Revolution and which were therefore distorted. In any case, history consigned these figures to the past once a soviet government had taken power. These assertions were not without foundation — which is not to say that Lenin would have agreed in any case to submit to another election. A fair analysis of events demands that one consider the fact that Russia was in the midst of revolutionary change, of disintegration and reorientation. The new battle lines which emerged in the wake of the Bolshevik coup scarcely had time to coalesce in the countryside. The mass of peasants who favoured the Socialist Revolutionaries voted for a party whose activist branch, the left SRs, had recently entered the new Soviet government. This fact was not reflected adequately in the results of the vote or in the mandate it conferred. The claim that the rural population voted *against* the events of October is without foundation. The vote also did not indicate any sympathy for Kerensky. The election cannot be understood either to have approved or disapproved a soviet republic: the most elementary pre-conditions for such a determination were lacking in many rural areas. The rapid pace of events, the dissembling of political goals on all sides for propaganda purposes and finally widespread apathy and confusion all conspired to render impossible elections of any real import. Elections indeed amounted to a mere momentary glimpse of a rapidly evolving situation.

The most significant results were to be found in the cities and in the army where political distinctions were most clearly drawn. A strong majority of workers and soldiers voted for the Bolsheviks. The liberal Kadets received substantial support, partly because conservative social strata fell in behind them. A consolidation process had evidently begun within the bourgeoisie which had lost its taste for Kerensky after the Kornilov revolt. Support for the Menshevik Social Democrats dwindled to its traditional hard core and there was little reason to believe that they would ever again rise to challenge the Bolsheviks. In his detailed analysis of the election,

siiskoe uchreditel'noe sobranie Pod. red. I.S. Mal'chevskii (Moscow–Leningrad, 1930).

the American historian O.H. Radkey has demonstrated convincingly that Bolshevik influence was spreading rapidly through rural areas as soldiers returned home from the front. Nothing could compete with the immediate measures offered by the Bolsheviks — peace and the redistribution of the land. The SRs continued to attract a majority but their support was soft and likely to evaporate.[9] The proportion of dedicated supporters they could muster not only to vote but also to participate actively in the political struggle was probably far inferior to hard core Bolshevik support.

Lenin's order to disperse the Constituent Assembly precipitated formal protests but no vigorous efforts to protect the democratic parliament. The security operation directed against the Assembly failed to spark the civil war which many had predicted. By the time of the swearing-in ceremony, calls for parliamentary representation had evidently become a hollow gesture for the vast majority of the population. The struggle for political power could no longer be determined by ballot papers and complex electoral procedures. Russia was in the midst of revolution and parliamentary democracy could not survive under the circumstances. Those who wish to engage in further conjecture might be well advised to be prudent with their conclusions. Right across Europe the parliamentary form of government encountered severe difficulty in the postwar years. This is especially true of countries where it first came into existence in the wake of the war.

The October Revolution had another important constitutional result. Not only fledgeling bourgeois democracy was destroyed but also the unique brand of parliamentarism which had developed in the soviets after the February Days. Soviet democracy had provided an opportunity for socialist parties of various hues to associate, but it too now fell victim to the Bolshevik seizure of power. This second consequence of 'Red October' also requires close examination. After the abdication of the Tsar, workers' and soldiers' soviets and, shortly afterwards, peasant soviets sprang up *alongside* the traditional institutions of state. These soviets represented a form of worker, soldier and peasant self-government in which the bourgeoisie could not interfere. Soviet institutions were viewed by their supporters as the organised expression of 'revolutionary democ-

---

9. The divisions and tensions within the Socialist Revolutionaries are analysed in the critical study by O.H. Radkey, *The Sickle under the Hammer. The Russian Socialist Revolutionaries in the Early Months of Soviet Rule* (New York, 1963) and also in Radkey's book mentioned in chapter 6, n.13.

racy', of direct democracy for the working people. With Central Executive Committees and All-Russian Congresses of Soviets, representative organs were created at the national level over and above the local soviets. These assemblies of deputies functioned in a highly parliamentary manner. An important feature of Menshevik and Socialist Revolutionary policy, however, was the desire not to replace the state with soviets but instead to enshrine self-government for the working classes in the forthcoming democratic, parliamentary constitution. This would give the masses strong institutional representation, free of bourgeois influence, and the soviets thus constituted would provide additional control over the activities of the state.[10]

In his 'April Theses' Lenin went far beyond this plan. The Bolshevik slogan 'all power to the soviets' implied that they would not simply exist alongside the state but would develop an entirely new form of government which, as the revolution proceeded, would displace and destroy the bourgeois government. The soviet state (or commune state as Lenin called it) would establish a dictatorship of the proletariat and the poorest strata of peasantry who had still to be attracted to the side of the working class. In order to do this the peasant masses would have to be weaned away from the influence of petty bourgeois pseudo-socialists and thus away from the bourgeoisie itself. As soviet government replaced bourgeois government, what Lenin called a transitional form of state would emerge on the road from capitalism to socialism. In order to perform their appointed function, the soviets would have to be 'restructured'. This comprised their being liberated and cleansed of those forces (most Mensheviks and SRs for example) which clung to parliamentary democracy and which refused to accept a soviet socialist republic in place of a democratic republic. To this extent, Lenin did indeed destroy the democratic consensus of the parties participating in the soviets. So far as he was concerned, a soviet republic was only of value if the Bolsheviks were at the helm.

As we know, other sections of the Bolshevik party imagined soviet power differently. People such as Kamenev and Zinoviev did not object to transferring all state power to the soviets, but they did not go so far as to wish to replace the democracy of the soviets (of which Lenin spoke as well) by the dictatorship of a single party. Of

10. For this and what follows see chapters 6 and 7 of this book and the comments throughout the standard analysis by Anweiler mentioned in n.6.

course, this grouping was also supremely interested in bringing the Bolshevik party to power. However, its leaders thought that political power should not be imposed on the soviets by means of direct action or armed insurrection. Instead, power should accrue legitimately to the Bolsheviks through majority decisions in the soviets. Political opposition organised into parties was thought to have an integrating effect within the soviets.[11]

Lenin was not totally averse to the idea that the political struggle might continue in a soviet republic. However, such opposition would not be allowed to organise or entrench itself in the soviets — the new institutions of state. Since the soviets would be identical with the new state without any separation of powers, they could hardly be expected to accommodate political opposition, according to Lenin. Those who did not repent and convert to the views of the proletariat as expressed by its vanguard, the Bolshevik party, would be obliged to quit the soviets. They would have to be considered class enemies and as such could not be tolerated. The seriousness of this difference of opinion became apparent in the discussions of the Bolshevik central committee about the reasons for an armed uprising. Lenin's opponents viewed Bolshevik power as based on a mandate from revolutionary democracy; for Lenin, however, political power was rooted in the party's own strength. This strength, Lenin believed, should now be bent towards aligning the soviets with the will of the masses and towards preparing them to fulfil their new governmental functions.

The Bolshevik *coup d'état* in Petrograd did not allay this controversy. Indeed it became all the more pressing. The second Congress of Soviets of Workers' and Soldiers' Deputies was not asked to depose the Provisional Government but was called upon to sanction the outcome of the uprising of the Petrograd Soviet under Bolshevik leadership. As a result of the disposition of forces within this Congress, finding a majority to support Bolshevik proposals and ratify previous events was no longer a prime concern: the Bolsheviks could clearly muster the necessary votes with the support of the left SRs. Of some 650 deputies, the old Soviet Executive could count on only about 100 votes. The Mensheviks and SRs had suffered disastrous losses and were riven by internal conflicts. The burning question became whether these political minorities should

---

11. See the literature mentioned in n.15 for the differences of opinion within the party.

be tolerated in the new Soviet Republic or whether they were, in Trotsky's celebrated phrase, 'miserable cliques and bankrupts' who belonged 'on the garbage heap of history'.[12]

The decimated Mensheviks and SRs protested vehemently and, with the leaders of the former democratic soviets leading the way, marched out of the Congress. They denounced the Bolshevik seizure of power, claiming it had been 'hatched behind the backs of all the other parties represented in the soviets'. It was a 'crime against the motherland and the revolution' which resulted in the destruction of the whole soviet system; it was a military conspiracy which thwarted the plan for a Constituent Assembly, increased the danger of a military catastrophe and served the cause of counter-revolution. Differences had obviously hardened into deep-seated hostility. The Bolsheviks and left SRs remained in the congress hall and confirmed without debate the decrees presented to them by the Council of People's Commissars. On 27 October (9 November) one could read in Gorky's *Novaya Zhizn'* that the Bolshevik coup had transformed the 'parliament of revolutionary democracy' into an institution 'which mechanically lent sweeping approval to the directives of the Bolshevik Central Committee'.[13] The Mensheviks and 'rightist' Socialist Revolutionaries formed an 'All-Russian Committee to Save the Motherland and the Revolution' — an alternative government which remained impotent. These parties were not the only groups however to refuse Bolshevik pressure to cede to the victors of Petrograd.[14] Links with socialist factions and groupings which might have been won over to the new Soviet Government were also severed.

Much of the sense of outrage would doubtless have been avoided if Lenin had been willing to leave soviet democracy intact and create a socialist coalition government instead of a purely Bolshevik Council of People's Commissars. Even within the Bolshevik central committee voices were raised in favour of broadening the political base of the new regime — for reasons of principle as well as political expediency. Only reluctantly did Lenin and Trotsky yield to these demands and permit discussions about a possible multi-party

12. Documents on the Second All-Russian Congress of Soviets can be found in *Vtoroi Vsesoyuznyi s-ezd sovetov. Sbornik dokumentov* (Moscow, 1957). For events at the Congress see Bunyan and Fisher, pp. 109ff.
13. Cited in Anweiler, p. 244.
14. S. Melgunov, *Kak bol'sheviki zakhvatili vlast'. Oktyabr'skii perevorot 1917 g.* (How the Bolsheviks seized power. The October Revolution 1917) (Paris, 1953), pp. 178ff.

government with non-Bolshevik formations, especially the powerful All-Russian Union of Railway Workers.[15] By the end of November, the only fruit of this effort was an attempted coalition with the left SRs who had already made common cause with the Bolsheviks at the All-Russian Congress of Soviets. By bringing a few SR commissars into the government the Bolsheviks gained an opportunity finally to penetrate the still hostile peasant soviets. However, even this limited attempt to form a partnership with parties enjoying equal rights and to continue with soviet democracy could not survive the spring of 1918. More precisely, it could not withstand the shock of the Treaty of Brest–Litovsk.[16] Even those who had done much to support the Bolsheviks were denounced as hostile, counter-revolutionary forces and expelled from the new Soviet Republic. Now that the soviets had become the organs of state, the Bolsheviks were evidently determined to smear any opposition within these institutions as traitors to the Revolution. No effort could be spared in stamping out all 'hotbeds of counter-revolution' as quickly as possible.

The Bolsheviks had had very little hand in shaping the world in which they now found themselves and the question therefore arises of what foundation Lenin and his supporters possessed on which to base their power during the revolutionary period. It is too simplistic to assert that the revolutionaries of October maintained power and extended their influence rapidly over vast expanses of the country solely by means of naked force, terror and bayonets. Although the role of violence and compulsion in the Bolshevik Revolution cannot be denied, this alone does not suffice to explain its triumph.[17] The secret of the Bolsheviks' success lay much more in the policies which they pursued. They managed to isolate organised opposition and cut it off from the general population. The masses — not only workers and soldiers but, more importantly, the broad peasant strata as well — came to identify their hopes for the future with Bolshevik policies. Typical of Lenin's strategy is the fact that he did not confront the public with a specifically Bolshevik programme. The

15. For the negotiations on a coalition see L. Schapiro, *The Origin of Communist Autocracy. Political Opposition in the Soviet State. First Phase 1917–1922* (London, 1955), pp. 70ff., Daniels *The Conscience of the Revolution*; also Bunyan and Fisher, *The Bolshevik Revolution*, pp. 184ff.

16. Radkey, *The Sickle under the Hammer* (New York, 1963), pp. 95ff., 203ff.

17. For the 'red terror' see G. Leggett, *The Cheka: Lenin's Political Police* (Oxford, 1981); for the Soviet view see P.G. Sofinov, *Ocherki istorii Vserossiiskoi Chrezvychainoi Komissii, 1917–1922* (Outline of the history of the Cheka) (Moscow, 1960).

major political decisions of the Council of People's Commissars were plebiscitary in nature and did not simply reflect the party programme. The Council immediately adopted the policies and promises which the various parties to revolutionary democracy had been proclaiming since February 1917 without ever having been strong enough to put them into practice.

The celebrated land decree,[18] ratified by the Congress of Soviets on 26 October, legalised instructions which the SR Peasant Congress had issued in August 1917 but which had never been implemented. The great agrarian reform — the confiscation of private estates including lands belonging to monasteries and churches — finally became law. The redistribution of land to the peasant and village communes, which had already begun in practice, was legitimised. The same principle applies to the Bolshevik peace decree, the most powerful document of its time.[19] It comprised all the old notions of a democratic peace: abolition of secret diplomacy, no annexations or indemnities and self-determination for all nations and peoples. There was nothing here to conflict with the statements which had appeared repeatedly from February to October in the peace declarations of the Soviet Executive; nothing which could fail to appeal to the broad masses. The talk was of democracy, not Bolshevism or the dictatorship of the proletariat. Specifically Bolshevik principles were not mentioned at all: the terms 'socialism', 'world revolution', 'civil war against imperialism', etc. were nowhere to be found. What was new was the suggestion that negotiations about an armistice and a peace treaty should begin *immediately*. New as well was the determination actually to withdraw from the war. Lenin had no need to seek a consensus with the politically organised forces in the old democratic soviets because he dared to do what under the circumstances had to be done.

18. Text in J. Bunyan and H.H. Fisher, *The Bolshevik Revolution 1917–1918: Documents and Material* (Stanford, 1961), pp. 129ff.
19. Ibid., pp. 312–15.

10

Early Soviet Government

In the late autumn and winter of 1917 the Bolshevik party was still not firmly entrenched in power.[1] What strength it had derived primarily from the fact that no other organised forces existed that could pose a challenge. Lenin and his colleagues realised that their coup was not secure simply because the Provisional Government had been overthrown, the Constituent Assembly dissolved and soviet democracy restructured: their victory required political reinforcement. This was, however, more easily said than done. The Bolsheviks had little room for manoeuvre during the early days and the stabilisation of power dominated all other concerns. Certain measures imposed themselves on the government and few genuine alternatives existed. The first decrees of the new Soviet government demonstrated that the party could not and did not wish to impose anything on the country that would have disaffected the broad masses. Free rein was therefore given to the spontaneous, radical-democratic desires of the workers, soldiers and poor peasants — desires which had been harboured throughout the Revolution without ever having been satisfied. The Bolshevik government opened the floodgates to this largely undirected craving for change as probably the only available means to rally support and neutralise opponents. Steps were taken to legalise the redistribution of land, though in practice the agrarian revolution had become a lawless upheaval which no people's commissar could have overseen or controlled. Rural Russia was left writing in a maelstrom which destroyed the last vestiges of state authority still remaining after the February Revolution.[2] No one knew whether the authority of the new Soviet state could ultimately be extended to this disorganised

1. For the early days of the Soviet Republic see the authoritative analysis of E.H. Carr, *The Bolshevik Revolution, 1917–23* (London, 1950–3), vols. 1–3 and H.W. Chamberlin, *The Russian Revolution* (2 vols., New York, 1947).
2. Carr, vol. 2, pp. 28ff., Bunyan and Fisher, *The Bolshevik Revolution*, pp. 332ff.

and often chaotic process. At most, attempts were made to steer the restructuring in certain directions and to strengthen the local soviets so that they could function as disciplining bodies.

The Bolsheviks' policy towards industrial workers was very similar to their approach in rural areas:[3] the liberation of spontaneous revolutionary enthusiasm took precedence over all other considerations. The decree on workers' control of 14 (27) November awarded the factory committees (which had existed ever since February) full rights to self-determination: that is, direct control over factory management, the right to set production levels, supervise purchasing and selling and so on. Prior to October, combined opposition from management and government had always held these demands in check.[4] Traditional property ownership did not collapse immediately as it had done in the countryside, but the old elites evaporated. Workers' control in the factories did not at all lead to Bolshevik control. The first consequence of workers' control was that production ground to a complete halt in many industries. At best the workers developed a type of personal requirements economy in the factories which they controlled and a primitive direct distribution system which replaced the exchange of goods on the open market. It was not yet clear whether this type of reorganisation could be tied to the local soviets and subordinated to the central institutions of state. Developing even a modest socialist economy from this starting point posed an enormous problem. The Central Economic Council was charged with attaining this goal, but the power to do so was not so easily acquired.

The military was the third great sector which commanded attention and again the Bolsheviks adopted the same fundamental approach as on industrial policy and the peasant question.[5] The orders issued by the Council of People's Commissars to the army and navy in the first few weeks after the October Revolution were not conducive to stabilising the situation. Instead they furthered the process of decomposition which was already underway, not least because of the land decree which attracted peasant soldiers back to

---

3. For what follows see R. Lorenz, *Anfänge der bolschewistischen Industriepolitik* (Cologne, 1965), Lorenz, 'Wirtschaftspolitische Alternativen der Sowjetmacht im Frühjahr und Sommer 1918', *Jahrbücher für Geschichte Osteuropas* 15 (1967), pp. 209ff. For an overview of Soviet historiography on this subject see T.A. Ignatenko in *Istoriya SSSR* (1967), no. 4, pp. 3–18.
4. The decree on workers' control can be found in Bunyan and Fisher, pp. 308ff.
5. Cf. the article by J. Erickson in R. Pipes (ed.), *Revolutionary Russia* (Cambridge, Mass., 1968), pp. 224–56.

their villages. The Soviet government made no effort to halt the widespread disintegration of the army, partly because any such attempt would have been hopeless. Official decrees sanctioned the radical democratisation of all military ranks, thus strengthening the policy which the Petrograd Soviet had initiated in February 1917 with its celebrated Order No. 1 — a policy which the Provisional Government had of course attempted to rescind step by step. A decree issued on 16 (27) December proclaimed:

> Full power of command in every unit is vested in the corresponding soldiers' committee and soviet. Elections will be held to the military command and to all ranks. Commanders up to and including the regimental level will be elected by means of a universal vote of their units.[6]

This amounted under the circumstances to a dismantling of the traditional organisation of the army. The demobilisation measures which followed confirmed the Bolsheviks' disregard for the old army structure. The immediate consequence of these steps was an urgent need for an official armistice and a peace treaty. In the name of the traditional demand to arm the people or the working masses the army was integrated into the state apparatus — an apparatus which was, however, being destroyed. Slogans about arming the people provided a rationale for a process which the Bolsheviks tolerated and even furthered, though they had not initiated it. No one was certain whether the 'armed people' could be mobilised and deployed in defence of the Soviet Republic. When Trotsky set about forging the Red Army of workers and peasants in 1918, a very different structure was chosen and the revolutionary militia was supplanted by a conventional army.[7]

There was obviously a certain method to Bolshevik policy in late 1917 — even if the term 'policy' seems somewhat inappropriate. Lenin's thesis that the proletariat must first smash the old machinery of state was put into practice immediately after Red October. One could even say that the theory worked spontaneously since the party's role as a guiding and motivating force was limited. The Bolsheviks still lacked a well-developed political apparatus and the

---

6. The complete text can be found in *Dekrety Sovetskoi vlasti* (Decrees of the Soviet state), (Moscow, 1957), vol. 1, p. 244f.
7. J. Erickson, *The Soviet High Command. A Military-Political History 1918–1941* (London, 1962), pp. 25ff., also G. Ritter, *Das Kommunemodell und die Begründung der Roten Armee im Jahre 1918* (Berlin, 1965), pp. 93ff.

mass support which they enjoyed should not be confused with a strong, effective organisation. Until 1919 the party operated from premises no larger than a moderately-sized legal practice.[8] The events which simply occurred and those which the Bolsheviks succeeded in precipitating stemmed primarily from an absence of central leadership and control. They were not the harvest of a carefully planned direction from above. The decomposition process had to be completed and the old state liquidated — something which the February Revolution had neither attempted nor desired. Lenin's opponents denounced this process as a surrender to anarchy and to the coarsest instincts of the masses. The deliberate instigation of chaos was also an indication, it was claimed, of a Germano-Bolshevik conspiracy. Lenin, the hired agent of the Kaiser, was allegedly fulfilling his assignment to destroy Russia. Insinuations such as this were absurd of course, but the maelstrom which enveloped Russia did seem quite capable of destroying everything in its path, including the power of the Bolsheviks themselves. The revolution was in danger of destroying itself and even Lenin's supporters could not be certain that the risks had been adequately assessed.

The Bolsheviks were in fact no less threatened by the violence of the Revolution than those governments that had already been disarmed and overwhelmed. The party attempted to compensate for its inability to steer events by means of carefully planned agitation and slogans well suited to the situation at hand. Its decrees in the form of exhortations, appeals and commands went out over the 'direct wire' to 'everyone, everyone, everyone'. It was unclear whether these policies, proclaimed to the public in ways never before imagined, would prove quixotic in the end. However, one should not forget the opportunities afforded by the situation. By intentionally fostering mass anarchy, the victors of Petrograd eliminated any opposition which might have coalesced under more normal circumstances. By undermining all authority, the Bolsheviks succeeded to some extent in consolidating their own. This was a highly provisional consolidation of course which betokened weakness rather than strength and the party could not remain in this phase of the struggle. Spontaneous revolutionary activity had to be checked and channelled as soon as its destructive energies began to ebb.

8. For the organisation of the party apparatus see Schapiro, *The Communist Party of the Soviet Union*, pp. 252ff.; M. Fainsod, *How Russia is Ruled* (Cambridge, Mass., 1963), pp. 131ff.

131

Even before he came to power Lenin perceived the soviets, the legacy of the February Revolution, as an institution which could serve as the backbone of the Revolution. The soviet network provided a mainstay against disorder — an element of stability and a new form of state. The Soviet Republic would rest on new, 'democratic' institutions which would burst the limitations of bourgeois society and initiate the great socialist experiment. In his famous pamphlet *The State and Revolution* Lenin asserted just a few weeks before the October Revolution that the armed workers would create a new kind of state:

> *All* citizens are transformed into hired employees of the state. . . . *All* citizens become employees and workers of a *single*, country-wide 'syndicate'. All that is required is that they should work equally, do their proper share of work, and get equal pay. . . . The whole of society will become a single office and a single factory, with equality of labour and pay.[9]

The 'factory discipline' which had developed under capitalism would be extended to the whole of society and every citizen (with the exception of class enemies) would participate in the management of the state syndicate. Lenin believed this to be possible because the functions of the new state would be limited to 'accounting and control', tasks which had allegedly become routine under capitalism. They had been reduced, Lenin claimed, 'to the extraordinarily simple operations — which any literate person can perform — of supervising and recording, knowledge of the four rules of arithmetic, and issuing appropriate receipts'.[10]

This transitional phase would prepare the state to wither away completely. Such a vision of the future demonstrates that the Soviet Republic was not at all understood as a hotbed of anarchistic liberty. The entire active workforce would be expected to participate at all levels of the new revolutionary order. Lenin believed from the very beginning that the *political* tasks of the new state would not extend far beyond the suppression of class enemies. The final goal was to transform the political functions of the soviets into simple administrative functions, into the mere 'management of

9. Lenin, *The State and Revolution* in *Collected Works* (Moscow, 1962), vol. 25, p. 473.
10. Ibid.

things'. All this had far-reaching consequences in actual practice. The first decrees outlining the machinery of the new Soviet state revealed that the theory was not meant to be utopian, at least not in this respect but was intended as a practical guide to action. The self-government of the armed people would develop into a multi-level organisation and supervisory system able to execute and delegate the political decisions which more highly placed institutions transmitted to those below. Soviet democracy entered the model only in the permission given to function as a subordinate administration. This was made perfectly clear in directions issued on 22 December (4 January) by the People's Commissariat of the Interior:

> The Soviets of Workers', Soldiers', Peasants' and Poor Rural Workers' Deputies are the regional organs of state responsible for all questions of a local nature. However, they always act in accordance with the decrees and regulations emanating from both the central Soviet and larger formations to which they belong. . . . The soviets put all decrees and regulations of the central authority into practice through administrative channels. They take measures to inform the population of these regulations, issue appropriate instructions, requisition and confiscate, impose penalties, forbid counter-revolutionary publications, make arrests and dissolve social groups that foment active resistance or conflict with soviet authorities. . . .[11]

This assumed the de-politicisation of the soviets and the transfer of decision-making powers to the Bolshevik party.[12] The soviets, the democratic voice of the working people, were thus relegated to purely administrative tasks. No less affected, however, was the Bolshevik party itself which had grown by leaps and bounds after the October Revolution. The transfer of political power from the soviets to the party doubtless created a serious problem because the party lacked a powerful administrative apparatus of its own with which to manage the state institutions. As long as this was the case, the soviets themselves had to be transformed into the instrument of party management. To this end, the Bolshevik party entered the soviets and gave up its separate existence outside them. One can even speak of a fusion of the party and the soviets in the early days. Only by means of concentrating all available forces in the central

11. *Izvestiya*, 24 Dec. 1917.
12. Anweiler, *Die Rätebewegung*, pp. 300ff.

and local soviets was the new state able to function, able to halt the process of disintegration and erect the young, tightly managed Soviet Republic.[13]

Most party members exhausted themselves with their administrative duties. As a result, the party as a whole failed to develop a strong political presence and was largely absorbed into the state administration. Consequently, no opportunity existed to discuss freely and openly the dictates of the party hierarchy. Neither could they be refined by filtering through the party's internal democracy. Those party members who became part of the administrative machinery of the Soviet state found their time totally absorbed by administrative duties, by social organisations of all kinds and finally by the Red Army. All their energies were expended in subordinate roles where it was impossible to avoid de-politicisation, castration as an independent political force and transformation into an instrument of the central leadership.

This was one of the reasons why the Bolshevik party, the supposed 'vanguard of the dictatorship of the proletariat', itself became subjected to the dictatorship of its own leaders. Lenin had developed organisational centralism when the Bolshevik party was still an underground conspiracy directed against tsarism, but this centralist approach survived 1917 and became the norm in the post-revolutionary period. The organisation suited to a secret society of professional revolutionaries was replaced not by a democratic party but by a bureaucratic oligarchy which endeavoured to exercise supervision and control. Most party members were removed from decision-making roles and reduced to functionaries. The party as a whole played no part in formulating policy and was itself carefully supervised as it watched over the rest of the country. The central committee retained sole responsibility to make decisions which reflected the will of the people, the proletariat and the party.

Rosa Luxemburg qualified this method of exercising political power and of withdrawing the dictatorship of the proletariat into the party's inner sanctum as the 'tragedy' of the Russian Revolution. It was, she argued, a perversion which crippled the democratic elements in the Marxist concept of the dictatorship of the proletariat:

13. For the Soviet understanding of the leading role of the party in the soviets see B.M. Morozov, *Partiya i sovety v Oktyabr'skoi revolyutsii* (Parties and soviets in the October Revolution) (Moscow, 1966).

In place of the representative bodies created by general popular elections, Lenin and Trotsky have laid down the soviets as the only true representation of the laboring masses. But with the repression of political life in the land as a whole, life in the soviets must also become more and more crippled. Without general elections, without unrestricted freedom of press and assembly, without a free struggle of opinion, life dies out in every public institution, becomes a mere semblance of life, in which only the bureaucracy remains as the active element. Public life gradually falls asleep, a few dozen party leaders of inexhaustible energy and boundless experience direct and rule. Among them, in reality, only a dozen outstanding heads do the leading and an elite of the working class is invited from time to time to meetings where they are to applaud the speeches of the leaders, and to approve proposed resolutions unanimously — at bottom, then, a clique affair — a dictatorship, to be sure, not the dictatorship of the proletariat, however, but only the dictatorship of a handful of politicians. . . .[14]

Rosa Luxemburg's analysis of the dictatorship which the Bolsheviks erected on the foundations of the de-politicised soviets is clearly correct. However, this description of the oligarchic power structure should not leave the impression that this outcome can be ascribed solely to decisions freely taken by a narrow elite. The young Soviet Republic was born during a time of crisis and emergency. It had immediately to face the problems posed by internal upheaval and reconstruction, as well as an external threat which was no less menacing. Russia was still at war and powerful German armies had pushed deep into the land. The Bolshevik Revolution was thus beset by a host of mortal dangers: foreign armies, internal enemies and the threat of chaos and internal dissolution. It is difficult to imagine how the Bolshevik regime could have stabilised and consolidated itself if it had been wedded to the principles which Rosa Luxemburg identifies under totally different conditions as integral to the dictatorship of the proletariat. The 'socialist democracy' which she recommended proceeded 'step by step out of the active participation of the masses', was 'under their direct influence' and subject to the control of the entire public.[15]

14. R. Luxemburg, 'The Russian Revolution' in *Rosa Luxemburg Speaks*. Edited and with an Introduction by Mary-Alice Waters (N. Y., 1970), p. 391f. For an evaluation of this article see P. Nettl, *Rosa Luxemburg* (London, 1966), vol. 2, pp. 697ff. For the relationship to the divisions in the party and policy differences see the excellent study of P. Lösche, *Der Bolschewismus im Urteil der deutschen Sozialdemokratie 1903–1920* (Berlin, 1967), pp. 117ff.
15. R. Luxemburg, p. 394f.

Under the circumstances prevailing in agrarian Russia after the October Revolution, this kind of socialist democracy would simply have encouraged mass anarchy and the kind of violent convulsions which would not likely have engendered political order. Reliance on the spontaneity of the masses would have meant abandoning power once again under virtual civil war conditions. It would have amounted to a renunciation of politics and a type of self-disarmament which could not have been outweighed by any number of revolutionary promises and radical-democratic declarations. From the beginning, the Bolsheviks felt obliged to do more than compose resolutions. They were compelled to take real political decisions and to ensure that the far-reaching consequences of those decisions were put into practice.

That the Bolsheviks were under heavy pressure was never clearer than when they drew upon their limited strength in the soviets in order to face the outside world. The world was still at war and it showed no inclination to leave revolutionary Russia unmolested to manage its own power vacuum. The Soviet Republic had no choice but to withdraw from the war — as much in order to extinguish the external threat as to establish Bolshevik power inside the country. It quickly became apparent however that the Republic would not easily be allowed to disengage from the conflict with the Central Powers. All the revolutionary pronouncements, manifestoes and proclamations could not hide its security problem and the peoples and governments of the belligerent states were not about to grant Russia a quick peace and general armistice in order to ward off the threat to the fledgeling Soviet Republic.[16] Neither the weakened German proletariat, to whom the Bolsheviks appealed, nor the peoples and governments of Russia's allies rushed to the Bolsheviks' aid during the winter of 1917–18. The celebrated 'solidarity of the masses under the imperialist yoke' failed to cause the revolution to spread to the West.

Only the imperial German government was in any hurry to accommodate the Bolsheviks — in order to force Russia into a separate peace on the eastern front that would satisfy German war aims and free troops for the war in the West. The Germans perceived the establishment of a revolutionary government in Petrograd as a unique opportunity; for no matter how clouded its future,

16. For this see Carr, vol. 3, pp. 9ff.; G.F. Kennan, *Soviet–American Relations, 1917–1920*, vol. 1, *Russia Leaves the War* (Princeton, NJ, 1956).

it obviously needed peace.[17] The Soviet negotiators at <u>Brest–Litovsk</u> were quickly acquainted with the harsh realities. The Germans insisted that Soviet Russia renounce Lithuania, Poland, the Ukraine and the Baltic states and that she withdraw Russian troops from Finland.[18] As spokesmen for the new, revolutionary Russia the Bolsheviks were hard pressed to save face. At the end of December 1917 they had already officially recognised Finland as an independent state and assured 'the peoples of Russia' time and again in formal decrees that their right to self-determination would not be revoked — even at the cost of separation.[19] However, the Bolsheviks had not imagined that these rights would lead to such a rapid decomposition of the Russian Empire. Early in the new year the Council of People's Commissars dispatched troops loyal to a Ukrainian soviet government to continue the struggle against the independent Ukrainian People's Republic which had negotiated a separate treaty with the Germans at Brest–Litovsk.[20] Finland too was in danger of being lost to the revolution. At the last possible moment on 1 March an attempt was made to draw up a treaty which formally bound representatives of a Finnish Socialist Workers' Republic to Soviet Russia.[21] In the end, the decision to accept the German diktat was not made easily and the dilemmas it posed became the object of long and bitter debates in the Central Committee.

17. For an overview and assessment of the literature on German war aims in the east — a literature which has expanded enormously since F. Fischer's *Griff nach der Weltmacht* (*Germany's War Aims in the First World War*) — see F.T. Epstein in *Jahrbücher für Geschichte Osteuropas* 10 (1962), pp. 381–94, N.F.14 (1966), pp. 63–94.

18. For the course of the negotiations see F. Fischer (n.17, above) and, especially, W. Steglich, *Die Friedenspolitik der Mittelmächte 1917/18* (Wiesbaden, 1964), vol. 1, pp. 232ff., as well as W. Hahlweg, *Der Diktatfrieden von Brest-Litowsk und die bolschewistische Weltrevolution* (Münster, 1960). For the reaction of the entente powers see R.D. Warth, *The Allies and the Russian Revolution* (Durham, 1954), pp. 196ff.; Kennan, pp. 218ff. For more recent Soviet accounts and reactions to Western research see A.O. Chubaryan, *Brestskii mir* (The Treaty of Brest) (Moscow, 1964). This work presents a few supplementary materials from Soviet documents. For the ensuing period of Russo-German relations see P. Baumgart's study of the documentary evidence, *Deutsche Ostpolitik. Von Brest–Litovsk bis zum Ende des Ersten Weltkrieges* (Vienna and Munich, 1966).

19. For the recognition of Finland's independence see *Dokumenty vneshnei politiki SSSR* (Foreign policy documents of the USSR) (Moscow, 1957), vol. 1, p. 71.

20. Besides the literature mentioned in chapter 7, n.7 see H. Beyer, *Die Mittelmächte und die Ukraine 1918* (Munich, 1956); F. Fischer, *Griff nach der Weltmacht*, pp. 440, 474ff.

21. Cf. Chapter 7, n.9. From a Communist viewpoint see V.M. Kholodkovskii, *Revolyutsiya 1918g. v Finlyandii i germanskaya interventsiya* (The Revolution of 1918 in Finland and the German intervention) (Moscow, 1967), as well as Kholodkovskii in *Novaya i noveishaya istoriya* (1967), no. 5, pp. 69–81.

A sizeable group within the party leadership favoured responding to the German terms with a 'revolutionary war' — a position which smacked of desperation rather than overweening confidence. Their plan for a *levée en masse* might have had a certain romantic appeal but it was unlikely to meet with much success in the field.[22] After the first round of negotiations, the central committee had already made bold to offer neither war nor peace. This strategy failed, however, despite Trotsky's stirring declaration:

> In expectation of the approaching hour when the working classes of all countries seize power . . . we are withdrawing our army and our people from the war. . . . We refuse to endorse terms which German and Austro-Hungarian imperialism is writing with the sword on the flesh of living nations. We cannot put the signature of the Russian revolution to a peace treaty which brings oppression, woe, and misfortune to millions of human beings.[23]

When the German High Command responded with a new offensive, the Bolsheviks soon realised that they could offer no effective resistance. Calls to defend the 'socialist fatherland' met with disinterest.

An agonising decision had to be made. On 23 February the Central Committee decided to accede to the next German ultimatum by the margin of a single vote — Lenin's vote, one might say. Again the debate had been bitter. Lenin denounced Trotsky and Bukharin and declared that those who refused to accept the German terms were in fact sacrificing the Revolution to the enemy. Trotsky for his part was prepared to envisage even the loss of Petrograd and Moscow in the hope that a refusal to sign the peace accord would focus the attention of the world on Russia. His response to Lenin was no less portentous: 'If we sign this German ultimatum to-day, we may be confronted by another tomorrow. . . . We may gain peace but we shall lose the support of the advanced elements of the proletariat.'[24] This resistance to the peace treaty was rooted in the fact that the Bolsheviks were being obliged for reasons of

22. For the disputes about the peace treaty see the minutes of the Bolshevik Central Committee: *Protokoly Tsentral'nogo Komiteta RSDRP (b). Avgust 1917–fevral' 1918g.* (Moscow, 1958), pp. 168ff., also L. Schapiro, *The Origin of Communist Autocracy*, pp. 89ff., and Daniels, *The Conscience of the Revolution*.
23. For Trotsky's posture during the negotiations see I. Deutscher, *The Prophet Armed. Trotsky 1879–1921* (London, N.Y., Toronto, 1954), p. 380f.
24. Ibid., p. 386ff.

self-preservation to accept a peace which strengthened rather than weakened the class enemy — an enemy to whose international defeat the Bolsheviks were supposed to be dedicated.

The Council of People's Commissars finally signed the Treaty of Brest–Litovsk on 3 March 1918. It was a bitter pill to swallow for the revolutionary wing of European socialism and especially for the German Left. Rosa Luxemburg described the treaty as 'the capitulation of the Russian revolutionary proletariat to German imperialism'.[25] According to the leftist paper *Spartakusbriefe* on January 1918, only the German imperialists would benefit — Hindenburg and the Pan-German movement. The separate peace would do nothing to hasten a general peace treaty and would prolong the slaughter of the imperialist war.[26] In September 1918 Rosa Luxemburg was still denouncing the possibility that the first hint of Allied intervention in Russia would provoke a 'grotesque mating between Lenin and Hindenburg' and lead to the 'dictatorship of the proletariat on German bayonets' — a 'protectorate of German imperialism'. This tragedy could only be averted, according to Luxemburg, by a mass uprising on the part of the German proletariat which would save 'the honour of the Russian Revolution' and its own honour by igniting a revolution in the back of German imperialism.[27] The views of the Bolshevik leadership were not significantly different. They knew that the nature and global significance of the Russian Revolution would be seriously threatened if it did not receive support from a successful revolution in Central Europe.

If the ensuing events are considered in this light, the consequences of the dilemma afflicting the young Soviet Republic become clearly visible. Socialism in the new Russia could not develop freely as long as Russia remained isolated and unable to take her place in the larger framework of a revolutionary world. The instinct for self-preservation was in conflict with the humanitarian principles of the Russian Revolution. In the ensuing struggle, the need to save the Revolution inflicted ever greater damage on these principles. The dilemma was probably impossible to avoid. In 1918 the Spartacus League urged the Bolsheviks to prefer death and destruction to a

25. R. Luxemburg, 'Die russische Tragödie', *Spartacus*, no. 11 (September 1918) in *Spartakusbriefe*. Published by the Institute for Marxism-Leninism of the Central Committee of the SED (Berlin, 1958), p. 454; also P. Lösche (n.14), pp. 103ff.; P. Nettl, *Rosa Luxemburg*, vol. 2, pp. 690ff.
26. 'Die geschichtliche Verantwortung', *Spartacus* no. 8 (January 1918) in *Spartakusbriefe*, pp. 406ff.
27. Rosa Luxemburg, 'Die russische Tragödie'.

pernicious security which discredited the name of socialism. However, one could hardly expect such selflessness for the sake of the honour of the Revolution. No outsider had the right to demand that the Russian comrades quietly abandon the historical stage. Acceptance of defeat would have meant flight and capitulation before the problems besetting the Revolution.

The end of the First World War once again raised hopes that civil war would break out across Europe and sweep the Russian Revolution and its aftermath along in a great international movement. However, lofty predictions of the imminent triumph of communism right across Europe and Asia[28] were soon lost in the dullness and poverty of daily life in Russia. The Bolsheviks recovered much of the old Empire in the course of their struggle against the White armies and foreign intervention, and they erected a federal state within their domains, the 'Union of Soviet Socialist Republics'.[29] The Bolsheviks remained alone with the Revolution, however, and the paths they pursued during the following years diverged more and more from the broad, international concerns of the early days. Surrounded by a hostile world, the revolutionaries clung to emergency dictatorship and failed to pursue the ideals of socialist democracy within the confines of their own country. The hallmark of Soviet history became not progressive democratisation but the consolidation of the bureaucratic system. The bright promise of 1917 was stifled by the straitjacket of Stalinism and 'socialism from above' destroyed the essence of the Russian Revolution. Its international ambitions were reduced to the mere expansion and extension of Soviet power.[30]

Sixty years on, there is little reason to regard Soviet history as a failure for which the Bolsheviks alone are responsible. A more fruitful approach might be to consider the extent to which Soviet history exemplifies the inability of all nations to break out of power structures that vitiate their principles — whether socialist or demo-

28. Cf. for example G. Sinowjew, 'Die Perspektiven der proletarischen Revolution', *Die Kommunistische Internationale*, no. 1 (1919), pp. IX–XVI. For the historical context see G. Schulz, *Revolutionen und Friedensschlüsse. dtv-Weltgeschichte des 20. Jahrhunderts*, vol. 2 (1967).

29. For the historical context see W. Markert, 'Der Osten zwischen Nationaldemokratie und Sowjetföderation', now in his collected essays and lectures: *Osteuropa und die abendländische Welt* (Göttingen, 1966), pp. 187–201.

30. W. Markert, 'Von der Oktoberrevolution zur 'Revolution von oben'. Zur politischen Struktur des Stalinismus', *ibid.*, pp. 96–121. Also K.H. Ruffmann, *Sowjetrußland. Struktur und Entfaltung einer Weltmacht. dtv-Weltgeschichte des 20. Jahrhunderts*, vol. 8 (1967).

cratic. In our era, the emancipation which the Revolution of 1917 failed to achieve has become a worldwide issue and a political imperative from which no one may be excused regardless of his or her political or ideological beliefs.

11

The Russian Revolution as a Contemporary Problem

In the last decades and especially in the course of the last few years exhaustive effort has been invested in researching and describing the prelude to the Russian Revolution, the events of 1917 and finally the impact of the Revolution on the formation of the Soviet Union. The harvest of these labours is now immense and statements to the effect that the Revolution marks an irreversible turning point in Russian history no longer require a learned footnote. All this research was and still is coloured by a further question; namely, the place of this turning point in the far wider context of world history. Historians who wish not merely to record events but to assess them and derive models from them must enquire into the significance of this revolution for the contemporary world. This opens up an enormous range of questions, few of which can as yet be answered with any certainty. The following discussion is therefore intended not as a catalogue of interpretations but as an attempt to describe the problems which surround this subject.

The international significance of the Russian Revolution does not strike everyone of course as an enormously complex issue. On the contrary, it appears very straightforward to those who share the beliefs of the original revolutionaries (who never doubted the worldwide significance of their victory) or to those who believe in the historical 'truths' on which the sons of the Revolution base their confidence in the future. According to the official Soviet interpretation, the Bolshevik victory of Red October introduced not only a new age in Russian history but indeed a new age in world history which will pave the way for the era of worldwide Communism. Karl Marx had promised that all previous eras would be transformed into a mere prelude to history and this belief has remained strong:

The success of the Great Socialist October Revolution marked the beginning of the end of all previous social systems based on the exploitation of man by man. The pre-history of the human race was completed, the realisation of true humanity, the era of socialism and communism began its glorious triumph. To have opened the door to this era is the signal achievement of the Great Socialist October Revolution, and this renders it the most momentous revolution in human history.[1]

These are portentous words. On the fortieth anniversary of the Revolution Mao Zedong acclaimed the achievements of the Soviet Union as 'the pride of all mankind'.[2] Today we know that the sons and daughters of the Revolution have begun to dispute their inheritance. In Peking the legacy of the October Revolution was thought until recently to be most truly preserved not in Soviet-style welfare socialism but in the 'Great Proletarian Cultural Revolution'. The mighty east wind sweeps October aloft and carries it westwards; what began in 1917 sees its consummation as villages and rural areas encircle the great cities of the world and as Asia, Africa and Latin America erupt in revolution and storm the metropolises of the rich. The intra-socialist discord which has already begun to appear demonstrates that even those who brook no doubts about the world significance of Red October are starting to question the fundamental meaning of the Revolution.

When one leaves the realm of those who identify the Bolshevik victory with the onset of 'true humanity', it becomes much more difficult to summarise the various interpretations. Non-Communist views differ enormously and trained historians tend to proceed with caution and professional reserve. Little is to be gained from hasty assessments and many a historian may well point out that half a century hardly suffices to arrive at firm conclusions about the significance of the Russian Revolution. A long historical perspective and broad overview were essential after 1789 in order to conclude,

---

1. A. Schreiner, 'Auswirkungen der Großen Sozialistischen Oktoberrevolution auf Deutschland vor und während der Novemberrevolution' in *Die Oktoberrevolution und Deutschland* (Akademie-Verlag, Berlin, 1958), p. 17. Cf. a Soviet account intended for a broad readership: G.N. Golikov, *Revolyutsiya, otkryvshaya novuyu eru* (The Revolution that opened a new era) (Moscow, 1967).
2. Mao Zedong, speech delivered in Moscow on the occasion of the fortieth anniversary of the October Revolution in *Die Presse der Sowjetunion* (Berlin, 1957), pp. 2818ff. For the 'cultural revolution' in China see the analysis of J. Schickel, 'Dialektik in China. Mao Tse-tung und die Große Kulturrevolution', *Kursbuch 9* (1967), pp. 45–129 as well as the documentation presented by K. Mehnert in *Osteuropa* XVI (1966), No. 11/12 and of L. Labedz in *Survey, A Journal of Soviet and East European Studies*, no. 63 (April 1967).

with Jakob Burckhardt, that thereafter 'everything was swept up in the age of revolution'. It is only recently, in the work of Robert Palmer for example, that the world (that is the 'Atlantic') dimension of the 'Age of Democratic Revolution' has been revealed in new ways.[3] In the fifty years after the storming of the Bastille little of significance was written with the exception of Adolphe Thiers' *Histoire*, though Carlyle's brilliant genre scenes and high moral tone were certainly inspiring. Nevertheless, we now know that Tocqueville's celebrated *Democracy in America* had already approached the very heart of the matter.

Despite all that can be said about the advantages and disadvantages of historical perspective one fact remains clear: widespread unanimity already exists regarding many aspects of the Russian Revolution, though opinion concerning its minutiae and ultimate significance may vary. Everyone agrees that the impact of the October Revolution extends far beyond Russia itself and that the causes and effects of Red October are enmeshed within an extremely broad historical context. The Revolution is acknowledged as an event of profound historical significance with important international ramifications. Historians are reminded time and again how deeply this great event affected and moulded the age in which we live and the questions which arise are concerned only with how this broad impact should be described in historical terms.

The bombast which often finds its way onto title pages is of little help. It tends to obfuscate rather than illuminate or provides only a vague, preliminary indication of deeper layers of historical consciousness. *History's Turning Point* was the title which the aging Kerensky chose for his final contribution to the year of his rise and fall.[4] More recently, German participants in the Great Socialist October Revolution demonstrated the assurance of eyewitnesses in entitling their memoirs *Weltenwende* ('World turning point'). At the same time, the West German Ranke Society published the proceedings of its annual convention on monarchy, world revolution and democracy under virtually the same title as these worthy veterans: *Weltwende 1917*. A glance at the contents will dispel any

3. R.R. Palmer, *The Age of Democratic Revolution. A Political History of Europe and America, 1760–1800. The Challenge* (Princeton, 1959).
4. A.F. Kerensky, *Russia and History's Turning Point* (New York, 1965); the numerous earlier, self-justifying works of the same author include: *The Catastrophe* (New York, 1927) and *The Crucifixion of Liberty* (New York, 1934).

notion that identity of title betokens increasingly identical views.[5] That there is nothing fortuitous about such portentous titles is evidenced by an outline of the *Handbuch der Europäischen Geschichte* (Handbook of European History) in preparation by Theodor Schieder: the seventh volume, set to commence with the years 1917–18, will focus on 'Europe in the Age of World Revolution'.[6] Even our colleagues in Moscow would have difficulty with such a title. Despite all the fundamental differences of opinion, a certain unanimity clearly does exist between historians in East and West — a unanimity which constitutes an important basis for the discussion which continues through and around the barriers which divide us. It is agreed that world history experienced a deep caesura when the Russian Revolution erupted — for whatever reasons — out of the tensions of the First World War.

So far as I know, it was Hans Rothfels, in his 1951 Tübingen lectures on 'Social Systems and Foreign Policy', who first attempted to provide a fundamental justification for the view that 1917 marked a historical turning-point and introduced an entirely new era.[7] He pointed to 'the two so momentously correlated events of the spring of 1917': the collapse of the tsarist regime and the entry of the United States into the war — events which cast the ideological and social conflicts of the time in a *universal* light. 'The western idea that the war was a social crusade' could now be taken seriously, according to Rothfels, as could the ideology which viewed the war as a struggle to make the world safe for democracy and to overcome the forces of darkness, reaction and autocracy. Wilson welcomed the new Russia because it accorded with his ideological framework of a union of democratic peoples. According to Rothfels, the October Revolution then unleashed profound new problems and set a landmark — like 1789 — behind which history could never retreat. New prominence was lent to class-warfare, as coloured by the Russian experience and the Wilsonian ideal of world democracy was suddenly confronted with the goal of international revolution. Thus 'the fundamental anthithesis between Moscow and Washing-

5. *Weltenwende — wir waren dabei. Erinnerungen deutscher Teilnehmer an der Großen Sozialistischen Oktoberrevolution und an den Kämpfen gegen Interventen und Konterrevolutionäre 1917–1920* (Berlin, 1962); H. Rößler (ed.), *Weltwende 1917. Monarchie, Weltrevolution, Demokratie* (Göttingen, 1965).
6. Th. Schieder (ed.), *Handbuch der Europäischen Geschichte*, (Union Verlag, Stuttgart); when the volume appeared in 1979 the title had changed to *Europe in the Age of the World Powers*.
7. H. Rothfels, *Gesellschaftsform und auswärtige Politik* (Laupheim, Württ., 1951) — text of his final two lectures. The following quotations from ibid., p. 8f.

ton' first became manifest. From a historical point of view, again according to Rothfels, the basic phenomenon 'of two fundamentally different social systems at the great power level has existed since 1918 and not only since 1945'. Consequently, the world is full of strong social and ideological cross-currents and lateral loyalties which are not blocked by national and cultural boundaries. This, said Rothfels, 'was the beginning of contemporary history'.

A little later Rothfels drew the consequences of his theory and began to interpret the term 'contemporary history' as more than a mere formal or chronological framework: instead he endowed it with a specific content and programmatical foundation.[8] One need not emphasise that since the 1950s this view has spread far beyond professional circles and has exerted enormous influence as a historically-founded interpretation of contemporary history. Among historians themselves, this emphasis on 1917 has encouraged some independent theories and divergent interpretations to emerge. Erwin Hölzle, for example, examined the policies of the great powers solely from the viewpoint of the history of ideas and developed a theory of the alleged confrontation of *two* international revolutions: one American and the other Russian. Both 'world revolutions' were the product of the historical experience of these powers situated at the edges of the old world and both the United States and Russia have been attempting to transform the world ever since first colliding in the First World War.[9] Those less familiar with Rothfels' views have at times arrived at misunderstandings or biased conclusions. Many believed that 'contemporary history' could be institutionalised and along the periphery of departments bearing this name events preceding the turning point of 1917 were often seen as a mere prelude to history.

Of greater significance is the fact that this view of contemporary history cast the Russian Revolution in an international perspective. It was portrayed as a momentous event with consequences at odds with the social thought, norms and institutions of the West. Hence the Russian Revolution appeared, even to traditional and conservative historians, as one of the great revolutions in world history. The antinomy of bourgeois democracy and the dictatorship of the

8. H. Rothfels, 'Zeitgeschichte als Aufgabe', *Vierteljahreshefte für Zeitgeschichte* 1 (1953), pp. 1–8.
9. E. Hölzle, 'Die amerikanische und die russische Weltrevolution' in *Weltwende 1917* (see n.5), pp. 169–84; cf. by the same author: *Die Revolution der zweigeteilten Welt*, (Hamburg, 1963) and his essays listed here.

proletariat, of Wilson and Lenin, of democratic socialism and Soviet Communism, of the League of Nations and Comintern, of democracy and totalitarianism, of the Eastern bloc and the free world was made to appear as the hallmark of the contemporary era beginning in 1917. It is an era in which human extremes and civil wars with ramifications far beyond the borders of the nations in which they are fought have become a daily experience.

The resulting emphasis on a bi-polar world did not, however, preclude awareness of the complexity of the contemporary age. Hermann Heimpel enquired, in the year of Stalin's death, whether the international and lateral currents described by Rothfels have not been engulfed by powerful vertical and nationalist counter-tendencies, especially by the heightened nationalism which manifests itself in non-European movements for emancipation from colonialism or from the imperialist hegemony of the great powers.[10] Today it can be said that the 1960s provided powerful evidence for this thesis and made it clear that the age of nationalism and nation states did not end in 1917 or 1945. Nationalist tendencies, which seemed to have waned in Europe, spread around the world and became one of the great, international movements of our time. The vitality of these vertical urges, described in such terms as 'pluralism' and 'polycentrism', seems not only to undermine the bloc system but also to transform it. New sympathies crystallise and traditional loyalties are revived. International visions of the future, fundamental sympathies and political interests have begun to free themselves from the bi-polar world of the superpowers. Civil wars have not only multiplied but have also grown independent of the view of mankind promulgated by the programme of the Communist Party or the Atlantic partnership. In Vietnam, Bolivia and the mountains of Yemen, in the tribal conflicts of black Africa and even in the slums of American cities, the Western model of democracy has lost prestige, or never had any, while the Soviet Communist model has little chance of supplanting it. Word has spread that the socialist system has not proven commensurate with its own principles and consequently the appeal of socialism is not strong. Many of our contemporaries view dollars and rubles, guns and napalm as interchangeable, regardless of their origins. Wherever protests or open rebellion erupt against oppressive powers, messages from the

10. H. Heimpel, 'Entwurf einer deutschen Geschichte' in *Der Mensch in seiner Gegenwart. Sieben historische Essays* (Göttingen, 1954), p. 171f.

147

Kremlin or the White House no longer inspire fundamental loyalties. Even the instructions that issues from party headquarters in Peking are not always welcomed and the little red book of the 'Great Helmsman' Mao Zedong was hardly intended for use as an instrument of neurotic self-glorification at hippy love-ins and communal happenings.

Hence the view of 1917 as a momentous turning point seems to have abated, as if the Russian Revolution were no longer seen as a grandiose event in contemporary history but as an occurrence in a bygone era. In the intervening half-century, even those who were most deeply affected by the October Revolution have suffered new catastrophes and fresh wounds. One is increasingly convinced that people of various generations and various parts of the world have highly different views of exactly when contemporary history began. The suggestion that 1945 should now be understood as the great divide between historical eras[11] will also fail, I believe, to overcome the inherent weakness in any universal definition of the contemporary age. However, the dead end which historians seem to have reached should not discourage them from inquiring further into the contemporary significance of the Russian Revolution. One should remember that it was modern research into social history and especially into revolutions which opened new horizons and induced us to re-examine our conception of historical eras. Interest has now shifted from turning point and forks in the road towards historical processes and structures which are necessarily of long duration. Sociological theories have been incorporated, the discussion of methodologies has expanded enormously and historical problems are being reconsidered. In Germany, Werner Conze pointed out the worldwide revolution induced by the development and expansion of industry since the late eighteenth century.[12] The fact that the impact of industrialisation is not confined merely to the technical and economic sectors of society is considered highly significant. Conze claims that this international process spreads 'practical enlightenment' since industrialisation undermines many different structures and encourages social and political democratisation, in addition to its effects on technology and economics. This is what Conze means when he speaks of the 'modern world revolution' and one might add that the dynamics of this process make it appear to be

11. W. Besson in *Fischer-Lexikon. Geschichte* (1961), p. 269.
12. Cf. W. Conze, *Das deutsch–russische Verhältnis im Wandel der modernen Welt (Göttingen, 1967), pp. 10ff.*

a 'permanent revolution'. The structural approach to history unites social, constitutional, political and economic history and the history of ideas. The enormous benefits of this approach are obvious and it has been adopted around the Western world. The American term 'modernization' (including theories of development and infrastructure) refers to a very similar concept and it remains to be seen whether this more neutral American term should not be preferred to the loaded and often over-used term 'world revolution'. The concept of 'modernization' may yet prove more useful than that of 'revolution'.

In any event, historians must now learn to grasp the full significance of the movement which had its origins in what Palmer called the Atlantic revolution in the late eighteenth century and whose influence is now felt around the world in the form of both technical-industrial and a socio-political upheaval. The Russian Revolution, with which we are concerned here, has a place within this huge process. (A curious fact which one might note in passing is that East German historians are not pleased by what they call this 'imperialist theory of an industrial age' leading to a 'finished society'. Werner Imig, director of the Marxist-Leninist Institute of Greifswald University, claims that it is a sign of the weakness of imperialism that its ideologues, faced with an intensifying peace movement in the capitalist world, 'once again attempt to drop the Rothfels theory that the modern era began in 1917 when the United States entered the First World War and encountered the Russian Revolution'.)[13]

The increasingly widespread view during the last twenty years (especially in the United States) has been that the Russian Revolution of 1917 should be included within the modernisation process as a step towards worldwide structural change. The Russian Revolution and the transformation of the social and political order in the Soviet Union are therefore continually confronted with other examples of modernisation — not only with earlier stages in Western Europe but also with contemporary stages in Japan for example, or with later stages such as those now occurring in the revolutionary 'Third World'. Thus the German-born historian Theodor von Laue described Russia as the first great example of a developing country and the Russian Revolution as an 'outside revolution' and 'a new category of modern revolution' — a revolution in a backward

13. W. Imig, 'An der Schwelle unserer Epoche. Zum 50. Jahrestag der Aprilthesen W.I. Lenins', *Beiträge zur Geschichte der deutschen Arbeiterbewegung* 9 (Jg. 1967), p. 412.

country.[14] In this way von Laue differentiates the Russian Revolution and its political consequences after 1917 from revolutions in the West and especially from the French Revolution. While the latter was not entirely devoid of outside influences, according to von Laue, it did develop socially and politically from a truly French crisis. The Russian Revolution on the other hand cannot be imagined without foreign influences since 'the main revolutionary impulses' emanated from the West. This interpretation clearly has much in common with Hans Freyer's analysis of 'European history of worldwide significance', and it is far removed from such slight maxims as 'east minus west equals zero', if for no other reason then at least for the depth of understanding brought to the problem.

When viewed from this angle, the turning-point of 1917 takes on a new appearance and becomes integrated into a broad modernisation movement sweeping eastwards. Even within a purely Russian context the October Revolution becomes part of a lengthy transitional period. Instead of the traditional phases of the bourgeois revolution of 1905, the democratic revolution of February 1917 and the socialist revolution of October 1917, a more extended era now emerges with its own internal logic and its own struggle with vast structural transformations. The tsarist ministers Sergei Witte and P.A. Stolypin faced the same priority that beset Stalin's planners, a priority of the highest national significance between 1890 and 1930 and one which straddled the turning point of 1917: a backward, agrarian country had to be modernised and industrialised as quickly as possible. In response, the government pursued in turn the protectionist, market economy and socialist paths to technical and economic transformation. The 'revolution from above' that finally succeeded was wrought by Stalinist production plans which imposed methods and sacrifices that cannot be examined within the framework of this book.

One should not overlook the fact that this structural approach to Russian history is highly instructive in relation to present day problems. The view of Russia as a developing country opens up the issue of the political and economic alternatives faced by underdeveloped countries in our own time. There is a great temptation not to allow historical examples to lay waste a priori the hopes and dreams of these countries and I believe that we must be fully cognisant of the fact that contemporary interests are often at play in

14. Cf. Chapter 1, n.30.

research into the Russian Revolution, though historians themselves do not always recognise this fact. This is true of the controversy concerning the Stolypin reforms, and Walt Rostow's stage theory of economic growth is also an informative example, though not one that should be imitated.[15] One should also be careful, from a methodological point of view, not to lose one's sense of historical proportion when interpreting the problems of the Russian Revolution in the context of the developing countries of the modern world. The promise and limitations of comparative studies in this immense field have not yet been well researched and the impulses now stemming primarily from theories of economic development will have to be put to the historical test. We still often lack the necessary tools in order to do as Hans Raupach suggests and apply modern insights into macro-economics to past economic processes.

All this perhaps leaves the impression that contemporary research views the caesura of 1917 as fully absorbed into the colossal process of worldwide transformation and modernisation. It might therefore be appropriate to abstract our subject — the Russian Revolution as a contemporary problem — from the larger structural model and to return to our original question. To what extent has the October Revolution, a revolution which 'shook the world' according to John Reed, maintained its status as a turning-point in world history?

In this context, the interpretation of the Russian Revolution as an 'outside revolution' seems especially fruitful. When the Russian Revolution is assigned to the nexus of revolutions in backward countries, it is implicitly assumed that a *new type* of revolution appeared in 1917 — a form of modernisation that altered the revolutionary movement which had begun in the West in the eighteenth century. This transformation of the original model needs to be elucidated and rendered more concrete. It emerges in the failure of liberal parliamentarism and in the rapid erosion of soviet democracy. It appears again when the traditional notions of bourgeois and proletarian revolutions dissolved in the huge spaces of an agrarian society that lacked a solid middle class and even any modern social classes. As the Russian example first demonstrated, the social nucleus of this revolutionary movement is an agrarian revolt by the peasant masses while the political nucleus consists of action by elite minorities. The missing mandate from society is

---

15. Cf. D. Rothermund in *Vierteljahreshefte für Zeitgeschichte* 15 (1967), pp. 325ff.

replaced by the revolutionaries' claim to represent the interests of the vast majority of the people and the dictatorship of the party replaces the will of a people that has not yet adequately organised itself. Political power is consolidated by dint of emergency measures incorporating the general mood. The government then begins to create its own methods of bureaucratic rule. Its aim is to gain control over the liberated masses by means of the party apparatus and the wider bureaucracy, indoctrination and compulsory work in order to prompt them to participate in the party strategy for development and modernisation. The new society which arises supplies an array of services but its *raison d'être* becomes lost in the master plan for the future and the mounting need to ensure security and reinforce political power. One could say that the impulses emanating from the West, 'from the outside', were dissipated in the vast Eurasian zones of developing Russia. Ever since the October Revolution the modernisation process has taken on a new tenor and other, non-Western civilisations have begun to emerge. This impinges on Western history to the extent that these revolutionary convulsions return 'from the outside' to affect the old world. Even modern structural research considers the year 1917 to be a turning-point in the worldwide modernisation process and views the bi-polar tensions of the modern world as stemming from the October Revolution. This is true, however, not only in relation to centres of political power and ideology but also in relation to the two basic models in which the worldwide modernisation process finds concrete expression. The Russian Revolution, occurring in both Europe and Asia, should therefore be understood as a transitional form and an intermediary between these two models — with effects on the West as well as on the East. Thus the Russian Revolution is intimately related to both modernisation movements outlined above.

During the political and social crises of the postwar era, non-Russian Europe struggled with many of the same structural problems which Russia faced after the October Revolution. One could point, for example, to the failure of parliamentary democracy — a phenomenon which occurred in Russia in 1917 but which spread slightly later deep into Europe. In 1917, in the midst of a devastating war, non-Russian Europe was already greatly affected by the Revolution. The Bolshevik plea to transform the imperialist war into a civil war against imperialism was directed not only at the masses in Eastern Europe and in European colonies and exploited areas; it was intended first and foremost to prompt a revolution that would liberate the proletariat in the Western, industrialised countries. The Russian Revolution was commonly thought to be doomed to failure if a European revolution failed to occur and Lenin's theoretical writings show that he was convinced that a mighty, worldwide process of revolutionary emancipation was about to begin. The revolt of Russian workers and peasants would trigger a world revolution; a proletarian revolution in the West would join the revolt of Asian peoples in a great conflagration aimed at the single, common enemy: bourgeois rule, the capitalist world economy and imperialism everywhere. Mao's China until recently orientated itself according to this distant goal — though the product of the Russian Revolution, the present Soviet system, is now believed to have reverted to the forces that block the emancipation of poor, exploited humanity.

In summary one can say that the modernisation process which emerged between 1776 and 1789 under the sign of capitalism and bourgeois-democratic emancipation engendered a new type of revolution after 1917 on the periphery of Europe and in the European colonies. This new type of modernising revolution, which first surfaced in Russia, aimed to transform the world according to the master plan of small, elite groups. While its concepts, methods and goals originated in the older, Atlantic-Western revolution (especially in the socialist, Marxist and Communist movements), it also developed approaches based on the local conditions of each particular area. For instance, the notion of revolt against the ascendant powers of the old world plays a central role in this modernisation process and has even spawned a new methodology: revolution understood as liberation of the masses from imperialism. As this new type of modernisation spreads around the world all uniformity is lost. National traditions, cultural and intellectual heritages, political ambitions and economic factors are integrated and this creates opportunities which lend contemporary revolutions a far greater variety than were ever seen in the Atlantic-Western revolutionary movement. This new multiplicity will be one of the hallmarks of the contemporary era.

Marx and Engels remarked in 1850 that Chinese socialism would one day be to European socialism what Chinese philosophy was to Hegelian philosophy.[16] Today, from Havana to Rangoon a host of

16. Karl Marx and Friedrich Engels, *Werke*, vol. 7 (Berlin, 1960), p. 222.

further possibilities have emerged. 'When our European reaction-aries during their impending flight through Asia finally arrive at the Great Wall of China,' wrote Marx, 'who knows whether they will be confronted with the inscription *République chinoise — liberté, égalité, fraternité.*' Nowadays, we realise that both Russia and the 'reactionary' West fail to rediscover their own historical legacy when gazing at the Great Wall and beyond.

Select Bibliography

The following select bibliography completes the information given in the notes of this book. It concentrates on recent publications in Western languages.

I. General Works, Articles

Anweiller, O., *The Soviets: The Russian Workers, Peasants and Soldiers Councils, 1905–1921* (New York, 1974)

Black, C.E., (ed.), *The Transformation of Russian Society. Aspects of Social Change since 1861* (Cambridge, Mass., 1960)

Bonwetsch, B., 'Oktoberrevolution. Legitimationsprobleme der sowjetischen Geschichtswissenschaft', *Politische Vierteljahresschrift* 17 (1976), pp. 142–85.

Carr, E.H., *The Bolshevik Revolution, 1917–1923*, vols. 1–3 (New York and London, 1950–3).

Chamberlin, W.H., *The Russian Revolution, 1917–1921*, vols. 1–2 (New York, 1935).

Geyer, D., 'Oktoberrevolution', in C.D. Kemig (ed.), *Communism and Western Society: A Comparative Encyclopedia* (New York, 1972) vol. 6

Laqueur, W. *The Fate of the Revolution. Interpretations of Soviet History* (New York, 1967)

Mints, I.I., *Istoriya Velikogo Oktyabrya*, vols. 1–3 (Moscow, 1967–73)

Pipes, R., (ed.), *Revolutionary Russia* (Cambridge, Mass., 1968)

Stites, R., *The Women's Liberation Movement in Russia. Feminism, Nihilism, and Bolshevism, 1860–1930* (Princeton, N.J., 1978)

II. Russia under the Old Regime

Gerschenkron, A., 'Agrarian Policies and Industrialization: Russia 1861–1917', *The Cambridge Economic History of Europe* (Cambridge, 1966), vol. VI, pp. 706–800

155

Geyer, D., (ed.), *Industrialisierung und sozialer Wandel in Rußland* (Göttingen, 1979) (= *Geschichte und Gesellschaft 5* (1979), Heft 3)

——, *Russian Imperialism 1860–1914* (Leamington Spa and New Haven, 1987)

——, *Kautskys russisches Dossier* (Frankfurt on Main, 1981)

——, (ed.), *Wirtschaft und Gesellschaft im vorrevolutionären Rußland* (Cologne, 1975) (= Neue Wissenschaftliche Bibliothek 71).

Hosking, G.A., *The Russian Constitutional Experiment. Government and Duma, 1907–1914* (Oxford, 1973).

Mehlinger, H.D., and J.M. Thompson, *Count Witte and the Tsarist Government in the 1905 Revolution* (Bloomington, Ind., 1972).

Oberlander, E., G. Katkov, et al. (eds.), *Russia Enters the Twentieth Century, 1894–1917* (New York, 1971)

Shanin, T., *The Awkward Class: Political Sociology of Peasantry in a Developing Society: Russia 1910–1952* (Oxford, 1972)

Stavrou, T.G., (ed.), *Russia under the Last Regime* (Minneapolis, 1969)

Swain, G., *Russian Social Democracy and the Legal Labour Movement 1906–1914* (London, 1983)

III. Political Parties

Ascher, A., (ed.), *The Mensheviks in the Russian Revolution* (London, 1976)

Avrich, P., *The Russian Anarchists* (Princeton, N.J., 1967)

Birth, E., *Die Oktobristen. Zielvorstellungen und Struktur* (Stuttgart, 1974)

Fischer, A., *Russische Sozialdemokratie und bewaffneter Aufstand im Jahre 1905* (Wiesbaden, 1967)

Galai, S., *The Liberation Movement in Russia, 1900–1905* (Cambridge, 1973)

Geschichte der Kommunistischen Partei der Sowjetunion in sechs Bänden. Ed. by the Institute for Marxism–Leninism of the Central Committee of the Communist Party of the Soviet Union (Berlin, GDR, 1968–76), vols 1–4

Geyer, D., *Lenin in der russischen Sozialdemokratie. Die Arbeiterbewegung im Zarenreich als Organisationsproblem der revolutionären Intelligenz, 1890–1903* (Cologne, 1962)

Hildermeier, M., *Die Sozialrevolutionäre Partei Rußlands, 1900–1914* (Cologne, 1978)

Keep, J.L.H., *The Rise of Social Democracy in Russia* (Oxford, 1963)

Lane, D., *The Roots of Russian Communism. A Social and Historical Study of Russian Social Democracy, 1898–1907* (Assen, 1969)

Lösche, P., *Der Bolshewismus im Urteil der deutschen Sozialdemokratie, 1903–1921* (Berlin, 1967)

Radkey, O.H., *The Agrarian Foes of Bolshevism: Promise and Default of the Russian Socialist Revolutionaries, February to October 1917* (New

York, 1958).

——, *The Sickle under the Hammer: The Russian Socialist Revolutionaries in the Early Months of Soviet Rule* (New York, 1963).

Rosenberg, W.G., *Liberals in the Russian Revolution: The Constitutional Democratic Party, 1917–1921* (Princeton, N.J., 1974)

Schapiro, L., *The Communist Party of the Soviet Union* (New York, 1960)

IV. From February to October

Andreyev, A.M., *The Soviets of Workers' and Soldiers' Deputies on the Eve of the October Revolution, March–October 1917* (Moscow, 1971)

The Bolsheviks and the October Revolution. Minutes of the Central Committee of the RSDLP(B), August 1917–February 1918 (London, 1974)

Browder, R.P., and A.F. Kerensky (eds.), *The Russian Provisional Government 1917: Documents* (3 vols., Stanford, 1961)

Bunyan, J., and H.H. Fisher, *The Bolshevik Revolution, 1917–1918: Documents and Materials* (Stanford, 1934; repr. 1965).

Burdzhalov, E.N. *Vtoraya russkaya revolyutsiya. Vosstanie v Petrograde* (Moscow, 1967).

——, *Vtoraya russkaya revolyutsiya. Moskva, front, periferiya* (Moscow, 1971).

Daniels, R.V., *Red October: The Bolshevik Revolution of 1917* (New York, 1967)

Gill, G.J., *Peasant and Government in the Russian Revolution* (London, 1979)

Hahlweg, W., (ed.), *Lenins Rückkehr nach Rußland 1917. Die deutschen Akten* (Leiden, 1957)

Hasegawa, T., *The February Revolution: Petrograd 1917* (Seattle and London, 1981)

Keep, J.H.L., *The Russian Revolution. A Study in Mass Mobilization* (London, 1976).

Koenker, D., *Moscow Workers in the 1917 Revolution* (Princeton, 1981)

Pethybridge, R., *The Spread of the Russian Revolution. Essays on 1917* (London, 1972)

Rabinowitch, A. *Prelude to Revolution: The Petrograd Bolsheviks and the July 1917 Uprising* (Bloomington, Ind. 1968).

——, *The Bolsheviks Come to Power* (New York, 1977).

Smith, S.A., *Red Petrograd. Revolution in the Factories 1917–18* (Cambridge, 1983)

Wade, R.A., *The Russian Search for Peace. February–October 1917* (Stanford, 1969)

Wettig, G., 'Die Rolle der russischen Armee im revolutionären Machtkampf 1917', *Forschungen zur osteuropäischen Geschichte* 12 (1967)

Wildman, A.K., *The End of the Russian Imperial Army. The Old Army*

and the Soldiers' Revolt (March–April 1917) (Princeton, 1980)
Wittram, R., *Studien zum Selbstverständnis des 1. und 2. Kabinetts der Provisorischen Regierung* (Göttingen, 1971)

V. Early Soviet Government

Brügmann, U., *Die russischen Gewerkschaften in Revolution und Bürgerkrieg, 1917–1919* (Frankfurt on Main, 1972)
Daniels, R., *The Conscience of Revolution. Communist Opposition in Soviet Russia* (New York, 1960)
Debo, R.K., *Revolution and Survival: The Foreign Policy of Soviet Russia, 1917–18* (Liverpool, 1979)
Döring, F., *Organisationsprobleme der russischen Wirtschaft in Revolution und Bürgerkrieg (1918–1920). Dargestellt am Volkswirtschaftsrat für den Nordrayon* (Hanover, 1970)
Hanlweg, W., (ed.), 'Der Friede von Brest–Litowsk'. An unpublished volume from the work of a commission of inquiry from the German Constituent Assembly and the Reichstag. (Düsseldorf, 1972) (= *Quellen zur Geschichte des Parlamentarismus und der politischen Parteien*)
Haumann, H., *Beginn der Planwirtschaft. Elektrifizierung, Wirtschaftsplanung und gesellschaftliche Entwicklung Sowjetrußlands 1917–1921* (Düsseldorf, 1974)
Keep, J.L.H., (ed.), *The Debate on Soviet Power. Minutes of the All-Russian Central Executive Committee of Soviets. Second Convocation, October 1917–January 1918* (Oxford, 1979)
Lorenz, R., *Die Anfänge der bolschewistischen Industriepolitik* (Cologne, 1965)
Pietsch, S., *Revolution und Staat. Institutionen als Träger der Macht in Sowjetrußland 1917–1922* (Cologne, 1969)
Pipes, R., *The Formation of the Soviet Union. Communism and Nationalism, 1917–1923* (Cambridge, Mass., 1964²)
Radkey, O.H., *The Election of the Russian Constituent Assembly of 1917* (Cambridge, Mass., 1955)
Schapiro, L., *The Origin of the Communist Autocracy. Political Opposition in the Soviet State: First Phase, 1917–1922* (Cambridge, Mass., 1955)

VI. Biographies

Ascher, A., *Pavel Axelrod and the Development of Menshevism* (Cambridge, Mass., 1972)
Cohen, S.F., *Bukharin and the Russian Revolution. A Political Biography* (New York, 1973)
Deutscher, I. *The Prophet Armed. Trotsky: 1879–1921* (London, New

York and Toronto, 1954)

Getzler, I., *Martov: A Political Biography of a Russian Social Democrat* (New York, 1967)

Knei-Paz, B., *The Social and Political Thought of Leon Trotsky* (Oxford, 1978)

Vladimir Ilyich Lenin. Biography (Moscow, 1969; London, n.d.)

Shukman, H., *Lenin and the Russian Revolution* (London, 1966)

Tucker, R.C., *Stalin as a Revolutionary 1879–1929. A Study in History and Personality* (London, 1974)

Ulam, A.B., *The Bolsheviks: The Intellectual and Political History of the Triumph of Communism in Russia* (New York, 1965)

Index

Index

LENIN 83
85-92
102
123

Bolshevik program
88-92